Militarisation of Outer Space and International Law

This book analyses the current international legal framework governing military space activities, evaluates their lawfulness, and recommends new international regulations to prevent space militarisation.

Militarisation of Outer Space and International Law begins with a comprehensive analysis of the international legal framework governing military activities in outer space. Today, outer space is widely utilised for a range of military operations. After outlining these activities, the book proceeds to examine their lawfulness in accordance with the applicable international legal regime's rubrics. It also reviews the proposals put forward so far, both within and outside the United Nations, as well as the positions held by leading space powers and their allies. Finally, the author offers recommendations for the future, emphasising the necessity for the development of new international regulations to prevent militarisation from extending into outer space.

This book will be of interest to researchers in the fields of space law, international law, military law, and military defence law.

Umesh Kadam taught international law in various Indian law schools from 1980 until 1998, including the National Law School of India, Bangalore. From 1998 until 2018, he worked for the International Committee of the Red Cross (ICRC) in the legal and communication departments, mainly in Asia and Africa. Since 2018, he has been working as an independent consultant and visiting professor of international law at some law schools. Apart from space law, his other areas of interest are international humanitarian law and international migration law. He lives in the Western Indian city of Pune.

Militarisation of Outer Space and International Law

Umesh Kadam

Routledge
Taylor & Francis Group
LONDON AND NEW YORK

First published 2026
by Routledge
4 Park Square, Milton Park, Abingdon, Oxon OX14 4RN

and by Routledge
605 Third Avenue, New York, NY 10158

Routledge is an imprint of the Taylor & Francis Group, an informa business

British Library Cataloguing-in-Publication Data
A catalogue record for this book is available from the British Library

ISBN: 978-1-041-27449-0 (hbk)
ISBN: 978-1-041-27450-6 (pbk)
ISBN: 978-1-003-75442-8 (ebk)

DOI: 10.4324/9781003754428

Typeset in Times New Roman
by Apex CoVantage, LLC

To Aba and Mai, my parents

Contents

Abbreviations

ASAT	Anti-satellite
CD	Committee/Conference on Disarmament
COPUOS	Committee of Peaceful Uses of Outer Space
CTBT	Comprehensive Test Ban Treaty
DEW	Directed Energy Weapons
ENMOD	Environmental Modification Technique
ESA	European Space Agency
EU	European Union
FOBS	Fractional Orbital Bombardment Systems
GGE	Group of Governmental Experts
GNSS	Global Navigation Satellite Systems
GPS	Global Positioning System
ICBM	Intercontinental Ballistic Missiles
ICJ	International Court of Justice
ICRC	International Committee of the Red Cross
Laser	Light Amplification by Stimulated Emission of Radiation
Maser	Microwave Amplification by Stimulated Emission of Radiation
MILAMOS	McGill Manual on International Law Applicable to Armed Conflict in Space
NASA	National Aeronautics and Space Administration
NATO	North Atlantic Treaty Organisation
PAROS	Prevention of an Arms Race in Outer Space
PPWT	Treaty on Prevention of Placement of Weapons in Outer Space and of the Threat or Use of Force Against Outer Space Objects
PTBT	Partial Test Ban Treaty
SDI	Strategic Defence Initiative
SDIO	Strategic Defence Initiative Organisation
TCBM	Transparency and Confidence-Building Measures
UN	United Nations
UNOOSA	United Nations Office for Outer Space Affairs

Introduction

Man's venture into outer space is one of the most remarkable scientific and technological achievements of the twentieth century. It was mainly driven by military technology. The United States and the Soviet Union began developing ballistic missile technology immediately after the Second World War. Germany's success in developing rocket technology inspired both to pursue similar efforts. Germany had started work on rockets in the 1930s. The United States and the Soviet Union decided to utilise this technology to launch objects into outer space. Ultimately, on 4 October 1957, the Soviet Union successfully launched the first artificial satellite, Sputnik 1, into outer space. Nearly three months later, on 31 January 1958, the United States responded by launching Explorer 1 into outer space. The ideological rivalry between the United States and the Soviet Union ironically spurred these achievements. The hostility that arose between them immediately after the Second World War marked the beginning of the Cold War, leading them to compete for global supremacy, including in outer space. From the outset of space exploration, military ambitions have chiefly driven space programmes.[1] Although the race to place objects in outer space was mainly driven by strategic and security reasons, many civilian applications were also developed during the early days of space exploration.

During the first two decades of space exploration, the most common military activities conducted from outer space were satellite reconnaissance and military communication. Nonetheless, 'Project Defender' and 'Project BAMBI' were launched by the United States in the late 1950s and early 1960s to explore the development of space-based systems using new technologies for ballistic missile defence.[2] However, numerous obstacles

1 J. E. S. Fawcett, *International Law and Uses of Outer Space* (Manchester: Manchester University Press, 1968), 29.

2 Donald R. Baucon, 'Space and Missile Defence', *JFQ Forum*, Winter (2002–2003), 51–2. https://apps.dtic.mil/sti/tr/pdf/ADA526289.pdf Accessed 25 November 2025.

DOI: 10.4324/9781003754428-1

hindered the development of such technologies. That attempt was the precursor to President Ronald Reagan's 'Strategic Defence Initiative' – colloquially known as 'Star Wars' – programme, launched in 1983, which envisaged deploying anti-ballistic missile systems in outer space. During the early 1960s, the Soviet Union also began exploring ideas for anti-satellite systems to destroy or disable enemy satellites in orbit.[3] The United States and the Soviet Union carried out controlled nuclear tests in outer space to examine the electromagnetic pulse effect in the early 1960s.[4] Thereafter, over the following decades, both countries gradually expanded the scope of their space militarisation programmes to include global positioning systems for military use, anti-ballistic missile systems, anti-satellite weapons, and other capabilities, in addition to satellite reconnaissance and military communication.

Space militarisation and, consequently, an arms race in outer space are closely linked to the terrestrial arms race. Furthermore, today's terrestrial weapons systems are interconnected with and heavily reliant on military space assets for early warning, command and control, reconnaissance, geodesy, weather forecasting, and targeting, among other purposes.[5] As a result, some of the early bilateral arms control discussions between the United States and the Soviet Union addressed terrestrial and space weapons issues together. Another factor linking terrestrial and space weapons is the development of space-based ballistic missile defence systems. The complexity is heightened by the fact that some technologies have dual purposes; for example, technology used for ballistic missile defence can also be adapted for anti-satellite applications.

Most of the non-military uses of outer space, such as meteorology, global positioning, satellite communications, remote sensing, and commercial space transportation, have become vital for our day-to-day lives. Any military conflict in outer space that could disrupt the critical space infrastructure needed for these applications would have disastrous consequences for our electronic civilisation. Such a conflict would not only pose a serious threat to national security but also severely affect our daily lives, which depend heavily on

3 *New Space Economy*, 'The Secret Soviet Quest for Space-based Weapons', (27 May 2024). https://newspaceeconomy.ca/2024/05/27/the-secret-soviet-quest-for-space-based-weapons/ Accessed 25 November 2025.

4 George H. III Baker, 'The Nuclear Electromagnetic Pulse (EMP): A Brief Tutorial', *BePress, James Madison University*, (August 2011). https://works.bepress.com/george_h_baker/32/ Accessed 25 November 2025. Also see, Peter Vincent Pry, 'Russia: EMP Threat', *EMP Task Force on National and Homeland Security*, (January 2021), 2. https://apps.dtic.mil/sti/pdfs/AD1124730.pdf Accessed 25 November 2025.

5 For an overview of links between air, land, maritime, space, and cyber warfare, see generally, Jeffrey L. Caton, *The Land, Space, and Cyberspace Nexus: Evolution of the Oldest Military Operations in the Newest Military Domains* (Carlisle: U.S. Army War College, Strategic Studies Institute, 2018).

satellite communication across sectors such as agriculture, aviation, banking, finance, healthcare systems, information and communication technology, power generation, shipping, and more. Conflict in outer space could trigger a spiral of instability, leading to global insecurity and public disorder.

Therefore, maintaining peace and order in outer space is essential. The international law existing at the dawn of the space age was inadequate to address the new challenges posed by humanity's venture into outer space, particularly in ensuring order and preventing confrontation in this new domain. Recognising this and the potential dangers of an uncontrolled arms race in outer space, the United States, and the Soviet Union – the only two space powers of the time – agreed to and supported the adoption of a few basic norms for space activities in the early 1960s. Thus, in December 1961, the United Nations General Assembly adopted a resolution to promote international cooperation in the peaceful uses of outer space.[6] This was succeeded by another resolution in 1963 titled 'Declaration of Legal Principles Governing the Activities of States in the Exploration and Use of Outer Space'.[7] This marked the start of a new chapter in international law – 'Space Law'. Since the legal principles in the latter resolution were merely recommendations rather than binding obligations, most United Nations members, including the two space powers, supported their further elaboration and conversion into binding treaties. As a result, in 1967, the Treaty on Principles Governing the Activities of States in the Exploration and Use of Outer Space, Including the Moon and Other Celestial Bodies – commonly known as the Outer Space Treaty – was adopted.[8] It is regarded as the foundational treaty for international space law. This was followed by four more treaties until 1979. These treaties are supplemented by customary space law, which has developed from state practice, accompanied by *opinio juris* since the 1950s.

In addition to the specific norms applicable to outer space activities under the aforementioned space treaties and customary norms, general principles of international law, certain areas of public international law, and some multilateral treaties also regulate space activities, including those of a military nature, to some extent.

The current scenario

It was reported in May 2024 that Russia launched a satellite equipped with anti-satellite capabilities into low Earth orbit.[9] This development closely

6 UNGA Res. 1721 A (XVI), 20 December 1961.

7 UNGA Res. 1962 (XVIII), 13 December 1963.

8 UN *Treaty Collection*, vol. 610-I-8843.

9 Jeff Foust, 'US Claims Recently Launched Russian Satellite Is an ASAT', *Space News*, (21 May 2024). https://spacenews.com/u-s-claims-recently-launched-russian-satellite-is-an-asat/ Accessed 25 November 2025.

coincided with the United Nations Security Council's debate and discussion on a resolution concerning the placement of weapons in outer space. In April 2024, the United States and Japan proposed a resolution in the Security Council to reaffirm the obligation of all States Parties to fully comply with the Outer Space Treaty, including the prohibition of placing in orbit around the Earth any objects carrying nuclear weapons or any other kinds of weapons of mass destruction, and of installing such weapons on celestial bodies or stationing them in outer space by any other means.[10] The resolution was defeated due to Russia's veto, despite China's abstention, and the support of 13 members.[11] The Russian Federation was keen on extending the ban in the Outer Space Treaty, limited initially to nuclear or other weapons of mass destruction, to all types of weapons. Subsequently, the Russian Federation proposed a resolution to ban any weapon in outer space and on celestial bodies, which was defeated, as it secured only seven votes in favour, seven against – including those of three permanent members – and one abstention.[12]

In February 2025, President Donald Trump, beginning his second term in office, proposed the creation of a 'Golden Dome for America'[13] – a space-based missile defence shield programme.[14] It aims to establish a comprehensive anti-missile and air defence system to safeguard the United States against future threats from ballistic, hypersonic, and advanced cruise missiles, as well as other sophisticated aerial attacks from hostile states.[15] President Trump officially launched it on 21 May 2025, selecting a design with an estimated cost of US$175 billion.[16]

In November 2025, French President Emmanuel Macron warned that future wars would start in space and highlighted the threat posed by Russia.[17] He announced an additional 4.2 billion euros in funding for military space activities up to 2030.[18] So far, China, India, Russia, and the United

10 UN Doc. SC 15678, 24 April 2024.

11 Ibid.

12 UN Doc. SC 15700, 20 May 2024.

13 Initially, it was known as 'the Iron Dome', but later it was changed to 'the Golden Dome' probably to avoid confusion with Israel's similar but geographically limited programme known as 'the Iron Dome'.

14 Stephen J. Cimbala and Lawrence J. Korb, 'Trump's Iron Dome for America is Ambitious: It Also Has Some Serious Technology and Policy Flaws', *Bulletin of the Atomic Scientists*, (28 February 2025). https://thebulletin.org/2025/02/trumps-iron-dome-for-america-is-ambitious-it-also-has-some-serious-technology-and-policy-flaws/ Accessed 25 November 2025.

15 Ibid.

16 Mike Stone and Jeff Mason, 'Trump Selects $175 Billion Golden Dome Defense Shield Design, Appoints Leader', *Reuters*, (21 May 2025). https://www.reuters.com/world/us/trump-make-golden-dome-announcement-tuesday-us-official-says-2025-05-20/ Accessed 25 November 2025.

17 Space4Peace, 'The War of Tomorrow Will Begin in Space: Macron'. https://space4peace.org/the-war-of-tomorrow-will-begin-in-space-macron/ Accessed 20 November 2025.

18 Ibid.

States have conducted tests of direct-ascent anti-satellite weapons.[19] Along with them, some countries in Europe, Iran, Israel, and North Korea are believed to have space weapons programmes.[20] Against the backdrop of these developments, including the alleged launch of a Russian satellite with anti-satellite capabilities, it is timely to critically examine the international legal implications of the militarisation of outer space. This book aims to provide a comprehensive analysis of the existing international legal framework governing military activities in outer space, outline current plans for military applications, critically assess the potential legal implications of these plans, and offer suggestions for future actions to prevent major confrontations in this new theatre of war.

References

Baker G. H. III, 'The Nuclear Electromagnetic Pulse (EMP): A Brief Tutorial', *BePress, James Madison University*, (August 2011). https://works.bepress.com/george_h_baker/32/ Accessed 25 November 2025.

Baucon D. R., 'Space and Missile Defence', *JFQ Forum*, Winter (2002–2003), 51, 52. https://apps.dtic.mil/sti/tr/pdf/ADA526289.pdf Accessed 25 November 2025.

Caton J. L., *The Land, Space, and Cyberspace Nexus: Evolution of the Oldest Military Operations in the Newest Military Domains*. Carlisle: U.S. Army War College, Strategic Studies Institute, 2018.

Cimbala S. J. and Korb L. J., 'Trump's Iron Dome for America is Ambitious: It Also Has Some Serious Technology and Policy Flaws', *Bulletin of the Atomic Scientists*, (28 February 2025). https://thebulletin.org/2025/02/trumps-iron-dome-for-america-is-ambitious-it-also-has-some-serious-technology-and-policy-flaws/ Accessed 25 November 2025.

East Asia Forum, 'China Pursuing State Objectives in Astropolitics', (13 August 2024). https://eastasiaforum.org/2024/08/13/china-pursuing-state-objectives-in-astropolitics/ Accessed 25 November 2025.

Fawcett J. E. S., *International Law and Uses of Outer Space*. Manchester: Manchester University Press, 1968.

Foust J., 'US Claims Recently Launched Russian Satellite Is an ASAT', *Space News*, (21 May 2024). https://spacenews.com/u-s-claims-recently-launched-russian-satellite-is-an-asat/ Accessed 25 November 2025.

New Space Economy, 'The Secret Soviet Quest for Space-based Weapons', (27 May 2024). https://newspaceeconomy.ca/2024/05/27/the-secret-soviet-quest-for-space-based-weapons/ Accessed 25 November 2025.

19 *Infra*, Chapter 3, at 51–2.

20 Clayton Swope, Kari A. Bingen, Makena Young, and Kendra Lafave, *Space Threat Assessment 2025* (Washington, DC: Center for Strategic and International Studies, 2025), 15–6. https://csis-website-prod.s3.amazonaws.com/s3fs-public/2025-04/250425_Swope_Space_Threat.pdf?VersionId=orhySgjISemJLjhdQKKes2OVb35jwkU5 Accessed 26 November 2025.

Space4Peace, 'The War of Tomorrow Will Begin in Space: Macron'. https://space4peace.org/the-war-of-tomorrow-will-begin-in-space-macron/ Accessed 20 November 2025.

Stone M. and Mason J., 'Trump Selects $175 Billion Golden Dome Defense Shield Design, Appoints Leader', *Reuters*, (21 May 2025). https://www.reuters.com/world/us/trump-make-golden-dome-announcement-tuesday-us-official-says-2025-05-20/ Accessed 25 November 2025.

Swope C., Bingen K., Young M. et al., *Space Threat Assessment 2025*. Washington, DC: Center for Strategic and International Studies, 2025. https://csis-website-prod.s3.amazonaws.com/s3fs-public/2025-04/250425_Swope_Space_Threat.pdf?VersionId=orhySgjISemJLjhdQKKes2OVb35jwkU5 Accessed 26 November 2025.

UN Doc. SC 15678, 24 April 2024.

UN Doc. SC 15700, 20 May 2024.

UN *Treaty Collection*, vol. 610-I-8843.

UNGA Res. 1721 A (XVI), 20 December 1961.

UNGA Res. 1962 (XVIII), 13 December 1963.

1 Space law and military activities

The current space law includes certain norms that, directly or indirectly, impose specific restrictions on certain military activities in outer space.[1] This chapter provides a comprehensive examination of specific provisions of space treaties concerning military activities. The current space law is predominantly treaty-based. Alongside treaties, a gradual increase in state practice is contributing to the development of customary international space law.

Multilateral law-making treaties on outer space

Given the reality that man-made objects can be launched into outer space, in December 1958, the United Nations General Assembly passed a resolution recognising the need for international cooperation and underscored the necessity of legal constraints to ensure the maintenance of peace and order in outer space based on the fundamental principle of sovereign equality of all states.[2] This resolution implicitly heralded the subsequent legal developments, albeit with the concurrence of the then space powers. To begin with, it established an Ad Hoc Committee to examine the legal aspects of space exploration. Later in December 1959, the Committee on Peaceful Uses of Outer Space (COPUOS) was established as an intergovernmental body subsidiary to the General Assembly.[3] In 1961, the General Assembly recommended to states guidance on the exploration and use of outer space, stating that international law applies to outer space and that outer space and celestial bodies, although free for exploration and use by all states, are not subject to national appropriation.[4] The General Assembly, deeply concerned by the lack of specific international legal norms governing space activities, established a legal subcommittee of the

1 In this book, hereafter the term 'outer space' includes celestial bodies unless specifically mentioned.
2 UNGA Res. 1348 (XIII), 13 December 1958.
3 UNGA Res. 172A (XIV), 12 December 1959.
4 UNGA Res. 1721A (XVI), 20 December 1961.

DOI: 10.4324/9781003754428-2

COPUOS in 1961.[5] The legal subcommittee formulated a set of legal principles to regulate activities in outer space. The General Assembly unanimously adopted these as a 'Declaration of Legal Principles Governing the Activities of States in the Exploration and Use of Outer Space' in December 1962.[6] Setting aside the issue of the non-binding nature of General Assembly resolutions, these developments of the late 1950s and early 1960s highlighted the importance and need for further development of space law through binding treaties and the establishment of guiding principles to promote this process.

The Outer Space Treaty, 1967

This very first treaty on space law was adopted against the background of ever-increasing space activities by both the United States and the Soviet Union, and a deep concern, shared by many, that outer space could be used not only for peaceful exploration and activities for the benefit of mankind, but also to serve the strategic and security interests of the two superpowers. There was a palpable fear that, if left unregulated, this activity might trigger an arms race in outer space, posing a threat to many countries. There was also a genuine concern for the safety of astronauts, liability for damage caused by space objects, and the appropriation of natural resources from celestial bodies, among other issues. Both the United States and the Soviet Union realised the potential dangers of leaving outer space unregulated and agreed to cooperate in establishing binding legal norms to maintain some order in outer space.[7] As of 1 January 2025, the Outer Space Treaty has 116 States Parties and 23 signatories.[8] All the leading space powers are parties to it. The Treaty sets out several fundamental principles of space law, many of which have been expanded and articulated in subsequent treaties.

The Outer Space Treaty and military activities

Among other things, the preamble of the Treaty states that the parties recognise that the common interest of mankind lies in the progress of exploring outer space and celestial bodies for peaceful purposes, and express a desire to contribute to broad international cooperation in the legal aspects of the exploration and use of outer space. It also recalls an earlier resolution of the General Assembly from October 1963, which calls on States to refrain from placing

5 UNOOSA, https://www.unoosa.org/oosa/en/ourwork/copuos/index.html Accessed 25 November 2025.

6 UNGA Res. 1962 (XVIII), 13 December 1962.

7 For a detailed background of the Outer Space Treaty, see Bin Cheng, 'Le Traite de 1967 sur l'espace', (English Translation) *Journal du Droit International*, 95 (1968), 534–44.

8 UN Doc. A/AC.105/C.2/2025/CRP.9.

objects carrying nuclear weapons or other kinds of weapons of mass destruction in orbit around the Earth or from installing such weapons on celestial bodies. It also takes into account the November 1947 resolution of the General Assembly, which condemns propaganda designed or likely to provoke or encourage any threat to peace, a breach of the peace, or an act of aggression.[9] These references clearly indicate that the primary focus of the Treaty was on preventing states from extending the arms race to outer space.

There are two key articles in the Treaty that specifically address military activities in outer space: Articles III and IV. First, let us consider Article III.

> States Parties to the Treaty shall carry on activities in the exploration and use of outer space, including the moon and other celestial bodies, in accordance with international law, including the Charter of the United Nations, in the interest of maintaining international peace and security and promoting international co-operation and understanding.

The obligation to conduct space activities in the interest of maintaining international peace and security, as well as promoting international cooperation and understanding, is not strong enough to compel states to refrain from using outer space for military purposes *per se*. It appears more like a preambular aspiration rather than a binding legal obligation. The term 'peaceful purposes' appears in the second and fourth paragraphs of the preamble. Article III is partly declaratory and confirmatory, emphasising that international law and the UN Charter apply to outer space and celestial bodies. As will be evident later, there has never been any doubt about the extraterrestrial application of international law, including the UN Charter, to outer space.

In contrast, Article IV is more precise and directly relevant to military activities in outer space.

> States Parties to the Treaty undertake not to place in orbit around the Earth any objects carrying nuclear weapons or any other kinds of weapons of mass destruction, install such weapons on celestial bodies, or station such weapons in outer space in any other manner.
>
> The moon and other celestial bodies shall be used by all States Parties to the Treaty exclusively for peaceful purposes. The establishment of military bases, installations and fortifications, the testing of any type of weapons and the conduct of military manoeuvres on celestial bodies shall be forbidden. The use of military personnel for scientific research or for any other peaceful purposes shall not be prohibited. The use of any equipment or facility necessary for peaceful exploration of the moon and other celestial bodies shall also not be prohibited.

9 The Outer Space Treaty, Preamble paragraphs 8 and 9.

By prohibiting the placement of any objects carrying nuclear weapons or other weapons of mass destruction in orbit around the Earth, as well as stationing such weapons in outer space in any other manner, outer space has been partially de-weaponised. Some authors describe this as 'partial demilitarisation'.[10] Not surprisingly, the terms 'nuclear weapons' and 'weapons of mass destruction' have not been defined by the treaty. A key question that arises in the present study – and it is important to emphasise it – is whether the term 'nuclear weapon' as used in Article IV should also be considered a weapon of mass destruction. In other words, would a weapon that utilises nuclear energy for its operation but does not cause mass destruction fall within the scope of Article IV?

The author believes that the Treaty bans placing only those nuclear weapons that are capable of causing mass destruction in orbits around Earth or stationing them in outer space in any other manner. A well-established rule of statutory interpretation called *noscitur a sociis,* recognised in leading domestic legal systems, is relevant here. According to McNair, this rule also applies to treaty interpretation.[11] It states that when two or more words with analogous meanings are coupled together, they are understood in their cognate senses.[12] They take colour from each other, and the meaning of the more general is restricted to a sense analogous to that of the less general.[13] Furthermore, the phrase 'any other kinds' in Article IV suggests that the drafters regarded nuclear weapons as weapons of mass destruction essentially. If the clause had been framed as 'nuclear weapons or weapons of mass destruction' or 'nuclear weapons and weapons of mass destruction', the interpretation might differ. To substantiate the previous interpretation, it may also be highlighted that at the time of drafting the treaty, only nuclear weapons that caused mass destruction existed. McNair notes that there is authority for the rule that when there is a doubt as to the sense in which the parties to a treaty used certain words, those words should receive the meaning which they bore at the time the Treaty was concluded.[14] In 1967, nuclear weapons were essentially and exclusively weapons of mass destruction. Therefore, the author disagrees with the view that 'all arms which utilise atomic energy in accomplishing their intended purpose, irrespective of their size or destructive force, would be regarded as nuclear weapons', especially with respect to the Outer Space Treaty.[15] The Treaty on the Prohibition of Nuclear Weapons of 2017 does not define nuclear weapons specifically but refers to 'nuclear weapons and other nuclear

10 Bin Cheng prefers the term 'partial demilitarisation'. See 'Outer Space: The International Legal Framework', *Thesaurus Acroasium*, X (1981), 70.

11 Lord McNair, *The Law of Treaties* (Oxford: Oxford University Press, 1961), 393.

12 Peter Benson Maxwell, *Interpretation of Statutes* (Bombay: N.M. Tripathi & Co., 1968), 289.

13 Ibid.

14 McNair, *The Law of Treaties*, 467.

15 Stephen Gorove, *Studies in Space Law: Its Challenges and Prospects* (Leiden: A.W. Sijthoff, 1977), 86.

explosive devices'.[16] In policy circles, nuclear weapons are rarely discussed in isolation; they are generally considered a part of weapons of mass destruction alongside chemical and biological weapons.[17]

Given the foregoing, it is possible to argue that Article IV prohibits placing in orbit around Earth or stationing in outer space only weapons of mass destruction. However, a question arises – why did the drafters single out nuclear weapons from the general category of weapons of mass destruction? One plausible inference is that since nuclear weapons are the most dangerous and highly destructive weapons of mass destruction, they required specific mention and emphasis. This prompts another question: What are weapons of mass destruction?

A weapon of mass destruction has not been formally defined in international law. It is generally understood that weapons capable of destroying property and/or causing large-scale harm to human beings are considered weapons of mass destruction. However, there is concern that the definition will remain controversial and uncertain in the future, and its usefulness as an analytical category will be increasingly questioned.[18] This said, what exactly constitutes 'property on a large scale'? Does 'large' refer to the quantity or value of the property? Should it be measured in monetary terms, or in scientific, cultural, technological, or strategic significance? When it comes to human beings, how many people would be needed to constitute a 'mass'? These questions lack straightforward answers. Nonetheless, one could argue that a weapon capable of destroying several objects in a single strike qualifies as a weapon of mass destruction of property. Similarly, a weapon capable of killing or injuring multiple people simultaneously could be considered a weapon of mass destruction of humans. Usually, a weapon of mass destruction can destroy property and cause harm to people at the same time. Regarding bacteriological and chemical weapons, Gorove contends that such weapons would also fall under the category of weapons of mass destruction, even if they are used against a small group.[19]

From outer space proper, let us now turn to celestial bodies. Article IV contains clear and detailed provisions regarding military activities on celestial bodies.[20] Before we examine these provisions, a brief note on an inconsistency in drafting Article IV. There are four references to 'celestial bodies' in this article. However, the phrase 'the moon and other celestial bodies' is used in only two instances, in the first and the last sentence of the second paragraph

16 UN *Treaty Collection*, vol. 3370-I-56478.

17 Michael C. Horowitz and Neil Narang, 'Poor Man's Atomic Bomb? Exploring the Relationship Between "Weapons of Mass Destruction"', *Journal of Conflict Resolution*, 58 (2014), 509–10.

18 John P. Caves, Jr. and W. Seth Carus, *The Future of Weapons of Mass Destruction: Their Nature and Role in 2030* (Washington, DC: National Defence University, 2014), 10.

19 Gorove, *Studies in Space Law*, 87.

20 The term 'celestial bodies' is used here to include the moon, unless otherwise specified.

of Article IV. The moon is undoubtedly a celestial body. Therefore, the absence of the words 'the moon' in those two instances in Article IV may be considered a drafting oversight rather than an intentional omission. As will be seen later, the Moon Treaty takes a different approach. It clarifies at the outset that its provisions regarding the moon shall also apply to other celestial bodies, unless specific legal norms are established for them.[21] In the Outer Space Treaty, apart from Article IV, the phrase used elsewhere is 'the moon and other celestial bodies'.

The first paragraph of Article IV prohibits placing nuclear weapons and other weapons of mass destruction in outer space and their installation on celestial bodies. Accordingly, the entire outer space, including celestial bodies, is intended to be free of nuclear or other weapons of mass destruction. The second paragraph of Article IV specifically addresses celestial bodies. It requires states to use them exclusively for peaceful purposes. It forbids 'establishment of military bases, installations and fortifications, testing of any type of weapons, and conducting military manoeuvres on celestial bodies'. The deployment of military personnel and equipment for peaceful activities on celestial bodies is exempt from these prohibitions. Therefore, Article IV not only deweaponises celestial bodies but also fully demilitarises them. This article uses both a generic and an enumerative approach to demilitarise celestial bodies. A somewhat comparable provision is Article I of the Antarctic Treaty of 1959.[22]

1. Antarctica shall be used for peaceful purposes only. There shall be prohibited, *inter alia*, any measures of a military nature, such as the establishment of military bases and fortifications, the carrying out of military manoeuvres, as well as the testing of any type of weapons.
2. The present Treaty shall not prevent the use of military personnel or equipment for scientific research or for any other peaceful purpose.

This language is preferable to the second paragraph of Article IV of the Outer Space Treaty because it uses the terms '*inter alia*' and 'such as' when listing certain military activities that are banned on Antarctica. This indicates that the list of military activities is illustrative rather than exhaustive, and it remains open. During the drafting of the Outer Space Treaty, the United States sought to include language similar to Article I of the Antarctic Treaty; however, the Soviet Union opposed this proposal.[23] Bin Cheng believes that even in its current form, the interpretation of the second paragraph of Article IV in good faith suggests that no activity serving a military purpose is permitted on celestial bodies.[24] It is

21 Article 1 of the Treaty.
22 UN *Treaty Collection*, vol. 402-I-5778.
23 *Travaux Preperatoire* of the Outer Space Treaty, UN Doc. A/AC.105/C.2/SR 65, 11.
24 Cheng, 'Le Traite', 607.

hard to agree with the view that the absence of a definition of weapons of mass destruction might let states deploy weapons of limited destructive capacity on celestial bodies.[25] Another perspective, which is equally hard to support, is that even if a weapon is not installed on celestial bodies, it might be placed on the moon because the Treaty does not clarify whether the moon is a celestial body.[26] It is important to emphasise that such views are entirely mistaken, as the moon is unquestionably a celestial body, and the Treaty explicitly demilitarises all celestial bodies.

The final sentence of Article IV aims to promote peaceful use and exploration of outer space by allowing military personnel and equipment to be used for these purposes. Despite the clear, straightforward language and its consistency with earlier provisions and the overall spirit of Article IV, Fawcett has proposed a convoluted interpretation of this sentence to justify certain military activities on celestial bodies.[27] He contends that permission to use military personnel and equipment on celestial bodies also implies that such activities may include defensive actions, such as establishing stations for missile warning or satellite inspection systems, since these are regarded as peaceful.[28] This perspective is unacceptable for several reasons. As previously noted, Article IV completely demilitarises celestial bodies by forbidding all military activities, whether offensive, defensive, or otherwise aggressive or non-aggressive. The use of military personnel and equipment is strictly confined to peaceful activities and exploration. This is further reinforced by the practice of States Parties spanning nearly six decades. The key criterion for determining whether an activity or piece of equipment is military is its function, rather than its formal status.[29] The vital role of military personnel and facilities in peaceful space activities was also emphasised when the Treaty was drafted.[30] Overall, it is widely believed that the provisions allowing for the use of military personnel and facilities in peaceful space activities do not in any way compromise the demilitarisation of celestial bodies.[31]

The Outer Space Treaty requires state parties to use outer space for peaceful purposes. This is stated in the preamble, and Article III additionally obliges

25 M. Muskat, 'New Developments in Outer Space and Their Role in Increasing International Security', *Zeitschrift Fur Auslandisches Offentliches Recht und Volkerrecht*, 30 (1970), 117.

26 Rex Zedalis and Catherine Wade, 'Anti-Satellite Weapons and Outer Space Treaty of 1967', *California Western International Law Journal*, 8 (1978), 461. Also see N. M. Matte, *Aerospace Law* (Toronto: Sweet & Maxwell Ltd., 1969), 299.

27 J. E. S. Fawcett, *Outer Space: New Challenges to Law and Policy* (Oxford: Clarendon Press, 1984), 15.

28 Ibid.

29 Bin Cheng, 'The Legal Status of Outer Space and Relevant Issues: Delimitation of Outer Space and Definition of Peaceful Use', *Journal of Space Law*, 11 (1983), 103.

30 *Travaux Preperatoire* of the Outer Space Treaty, UN Doc. A/AC.105/C.2/SR.65, 9.

31 Manfred Lachs, *The Law of Outer Space: An Experience in Contemporary Law Making* (Leiden: A.W. Sijthoff, 1972), 109.

states to conduct space activities in the interest of maintaining international peace and security and to promote international cooperation. Therefore, space activities are expected to be carried out for 'peaceful' purposes. This was also emphasised in the 1963 General Assembly resolution that established certain legal principles for space activities. However, Article IV mandates explicitly that states use celestial bodies 'exclusively' for peaceful purposes. This means that activities in outer space would be 'peaceful', whereas activities on celestial bodies must be 'exclusively peaceful'. The first paragraph of Article IV only prohibits placing objects carrying nuclear weapons and other weapons of mass destruction in orbit around the Earth. Whereas, its second paragraph prohibits any form of military activity on celestial bodies. Does this imply that the drafters intended to permit certain military activities in outer space while banning all military activities on celestial bodies?

One interpretation, based on the plain meaning of the word 'peaceful', is that peaceful means non-military. This would exclude any activity serving a military purpose – whether offensive, defensive, aggressive, or non-aggressive – in outer space proper. Conversely, the other view, supported by the United States and many other states, is that 'peaceful' means 'non-aggressive' and thus includes defensive military activities.[32] The Soviet Union believed that 'peaceful' is equivalent to 'non-military'.[33] Therefore, in the early days of the Outer Space Treaty, it was observed that the notion of 'peace' has always been contrasted with 'war', and 'peaceful' always meant 'non-military'.[34] Some writers in Western countries also supported this view during the early days of space exploration.[35] Interpreting 'peaceful' as 'non-aggressive' has been justified on a novel ground: That it allows States Parties to retain maximum freedom for strategic activities in the absence of an effective verification system.[36] Bin Cheng has convincingly shown how interpreting 'peaceful' as 'non-aggressive' leads to illogical, unreasonable, and absurd consequences.[37] However, today, nearly six decades after the treaty's adoption, the

32 U.S. Department of State, 'Declassification and Release of the Confidential Document: Definition of Peaceful Uses of Outer Space'. https://www.cia.gov/readingroom/docs/CIA-RDP66R00638R000100160004-2.pdf Accessed 25 November 2025.

33 See generally, Emilio Jaksetic, 'The Peaceful Uses of Outer Space: Soviet Views', *American University Law Review*, 28 (1979), 483–506.

34 G. P. Zukov, 'On the Question of Interpretation of the Term "Peaceful Uses of Outer Space" Contained in the Space Treaty', *Proceedings of the Eleventh Colloquium on the Law of Outer Space*, (1968), 36.

35 J. F. McMahon, 'Legal Aspects of Outer Space', *British Yearbook of International Law*, 38 (1962), 360. Even in early 1970s Manfred Lachs supported this view. Lachs, *The Law of Outer Space*, 106–7.

36 Kunihiko Tatsuzawa, 'Some Observations on the Meaning of the Term "Peaceful Uses" in Space Law', *Proceedings of the Thirtieth Colloquium on the Law of Outer Space*, (1987), 94.

37 Bin Cheng, 'Properly Speaking, Only Celestial Bodies Have Been Reserved for Use Exclusively for Peaceful (Non-Military) Purpose, But Not Outer Void Space', *International Law Studies*, 75 (2000), 82–5.

practice of most states shows that 'peaceful' is understood as 'non-aggressive'. Thus, all space-faring states today believe that the obligation in Article IV of the Outer Space Treaty to use outer space for 'peaceful' purposes does not prevent them from deploying military satellites for communication, navigation, ocean surveillance, geodesy, and reconnaissance.

The Astronauts Agreement, 1968[38]

Deeply concerned about the safe return of their astronauts and spacecraft in case of distress or accident, the Soviet Union took the initiative by proposing the Astronauts Agreement as early as 1962.[39] Undoubtedly, the United States was not seriously interested in adopting the Agreement, as it had already developed an efficient network of tracking facilities; therefore, its need for assistance in emergency cases was not urgent.[40] The Outer Space Treaty already provided for assistance to astronauts, their return, and the return of space objects to the state in which they were registered.[41] However, in light of the increasing number of space activities, the Soviet Union suggested that a detailed regime be established through an independent multilateral treaty to address the rescue and return of astronauts, as well as the recovery and return of space objects.[42] Eventually, the Agreement, which has self-explanatory provisions, was adopted on 19 December 1967 and entered into force on 3 December 1968 after receiving five ratifications, including those of the three depository governments: The Soviet Union, the United Kingdom, and the United States. As of 1 January 2025, it has 100 States Parties and 23 signatories. All the major space powers are parties to it.[43]

The Agreement does not specify what constitutes a spacecraft. In its title, it uses the term 'objects launched into outer space', but at some points in the text, it refers to 'spacecraft', while at others, it mentions 'objects launched into outer space or their component parts', and 'space objects or their parts'. In the national space legislations of many countries, 'space objects' are generally defined in relation to the launch element and its functional aspects.[44]

38 Full title: The Agreement on the Rescue of Astronauts, the Return of Astronauts and the Return of Objects Launched into Outer Space, 1968.
UN *Treaty Collection*, vol. 672-I-9574.

39 UN Doc. A/AC.105/C.2/L.1.

40 Damodar Wadegaonkar, *The Orbit of Space Law* (Bombay: N.M. Tripathi & Co., 1984), 16.

41 Articles V and VIII.

42 UN Doc. A/AC.105/C.2/SR.76, 5 and UN Doc. A/AC.105/PV.49, 61.

43 UN Doc. A/AC.105/C.2/2025/CRP.9.

44 See generally, Christopher Hearsay, 'Comparative Study on the Definition of Space Object in National Space Laws and Its Legal Effect Under International Law', *Social Science Research Network*, (May 2012). https://ssrn.com/abstract=2072514 Accessed 25 November 2025.

The Astronauts Agreement and military activities

The rescue and return of astronauts, as well as the recovery and return of spacecraft, raise specific key issues in the context of military activities in outer space. Today, all major space powers are extensively engaged in reconnaissance from outer space. It is possible to envisage a scenario where a military-manned or unmanned spacecraft makes an emergency landing or crashes in the territory of a hostile state due to a malfunction. Assuming that the concerned states are parties to the Outer Space Treaty and/or the Astronauts Agreement, can the state that has found the spacecraft or its debris refuse to return it because of the possibility that it may contain sensitive data? In the case of a manned mission of a similar nature, can it arrest the astronauts and charge them with espionage? Or must it, in strict adherence to its treaty obligations, safely return the spacecraft or its debris, including the reconnaissance devices, astronauts, if any, to the launching state, regardless of its national security?

The Outer Space Treaty and the Astronauts Agreement both remain silent on such situations. Extensive discussions on these issues took place during the negotiation stage. The Japanese delegate raised the following issue:

> His Government had been greatly concerned by a recent report of tests being conducted by a certain space power towards the possible development of a 'fractional orbital bombardment system'. . . . The present draft agreement or any future agreement on rescue and return could not place an obligation on a contracting party to recover and return a space object intended primarily for the development of a bombardment system to be placed into any kind of orbit, whether fractional or non-fractional.[45]

Similarly, the draft submitted by the Soviet Union in 1964 limited the duty to return space objects launched for 'peaceful purposes' to be determined, presumably, by the state in whose territory the space object or parts thereof land.[46] Due to opposition to this suggestion, the Soviet Union substituted reference to 'objects launched for peaceful purposes' with 'objects launched in compliance with the Declaration of Legal Principles' adopted by the General Assembly in 1963.[47] The United States opposed this proposal because the reference to the Declaration was indirectly meant to imply the same as an object launched for peaceful purposes.[48] Mexico also pointed out that, in the absence of any possibility of arbitration or reference to the International Court

45 UN Doc. A/AC.105/C.2/SR. 86.

46 UN Doc. A/AC 105/C.2/L.2/Rev. 1.

47 Paul G. Dembling and Daniel M. Arons, 'Space Law and the United Nations: The Work of the Legal Subcommittee of the United Nations Committee on the Peaceful Uses of Outer Space', *Journal of Air Law and Commerce*, 32 (1966), 343.

48 Ibid., 344.

of Justice, no reliance can be placed on the subjective determination of any particular state regarding the purpose of the launch.[49] It has been suggested that, in the absence of subsequent state practice to recover and return those space objects that perform surveillance upon controlled re-entry, it can be inferred that there is no obligation to recover and return such objects under the Astronauts Agreement.[50] However, the issue with the reliability of such state practice is that states are unlikely to admit that their space object, which has crashed into another state's territory, was involved in military activity.

Regarding the rescue and return of astronauts, the Soviet Union, Romania, and Bulgaria asserted that if launches are not in accordance with the Declaration of Legal Principles, astronauts who land in another state may be considered as spies or prisoners of war.[51] Bulgaria additionally stated that the obligation to rescue and return astronauts must be understood within the context of the entire Declaration of Legal Principles, and astronauts engaged in military activities could scarcely be considered as 'envoys of mankind'.[52] Incidentally, the Agreement does not define the term 'personnel of a spacecraft'.[53]

Eventually, a compromise was reached, and the Soviet Union dropped its insistence on including a reference to objects launched either for peaceful purposes or in compliance with the Declaration of Legal Principles, presumably because it was eager to secure an agreement quickly. Thus, in its current form, it seems hard to deny that the obligation under the Agreement to return space objects, as well as personnel thereof, is absolute and unconditional.[54] It has rightly been pointed out that the words 'all personnel' as used in the Agreement leave no room for distinguishing between military and civilian personnel.[55] Can a state refuse to return a space object or its component parts if it was launched in violation of Article IV of the Outer Space Treaty by attempting to deploy nuclear weapons or other weapons of mass destruction in outer space, or by engaging in any military activity on celestial bodies? Without independent and objective international verification, the obligation in the Astronauts Agreement is likely to take precedence. In such cases, the aggrieved state may

49 Ibid.

50 Tejas Bhardwaj and Tanushri Joshi, 'Analyzing the Obligation to Recover and Return Space Objects Upon Controlled Re-Entry Under International Space Law', *Paper Presented at the 74th International Astronautical Congress, Baku, Azerbaijan*, (2–6 October 2023), 7. https://iafastro.directory/iac/archive/browse/IAC-23/E7/1/77008/ Accessed 25 November 2025.

51 Dembling, 'Space Law and the United Nations', 345.

52 Ibid., 346.

53 It is curious to note that the title talks about 'the Agreement on the Rescue of Astronauts . . .' but the word 'astronauts' is nowhere used in the text of the Agreement. Instead, the term 'personnel of spacecraft' is used.

54 Bin Cheng, 'The 1968 Astronauts Agreement or How Not to Make a Treaty', *Yearbook of World Affairs*, 23 (1969), 205–6.

55 Walter D. Reed and Robert W. Norris, 'Military Uses of the Space Shuttle', *Akron Law Review*, 13 (1980), 687.

lodge complaints with the United Nations Security Council and COPUOS, and bring the alleged breach of the Outer Space Treaty to the attention of the international community.

The Liability Convention, 1972[56]

In response to widespread concern over space accidents, the Liability Convention establishes a legal framework for providing monetary compensation to victims of such incidents. It was considered and negotiated by the Legal Subcommittee of COPUOS from 1963 to 1972. An agreement was reached at the General Assembly in 1971, and the Convention entered into force in September 1972.[57] As of 1 January 2025, it has 100 States Parties and 18 signatories.[58] All leading space powers are parties to it. The basic provision of the Outer Space Treaty concerning liability for space accidents is further elaborated in this Convention.[59] The Liability Convention contains numerous provisions regarding situations where a space object causes damage to other states or their persons, natural as well as legal, and/or their property. The scope and purpose of the Convention's provisions indicate that its scheme is based on two distinct principles of liability: Firstly, the principle of absolute liability for damage caused on the surface of the Earth or to an aircraft in flight; and secondly, the principle of fault liability for damage caused to a space object, persons, or property on board, while it is elsewhere than on the surface of the Earth or its airspace. Without going into further details, it suffices to say that the Convention sets out procedures for settling claims, criteria for calculating compensation, apportionment of compensation when two or more space objects of different states cause damage, and liability of international organisations, and so forth.

The Liability Convention and military activities

Article I of the Convention defines a space object as follows:

> The term 'space object' includes component parts of a space object as well as its launch vehicle and parts thereof.

This definition applies to both civilian and military space objects. Therefore, if a reconnaissance satellite of a state sustains damage while in outer space

56 Full title: The Convention on International Liability for Damage Caused by Space Objects, 1972.UN *Treaty Collection*, vol. 961-I-13810.

57 UNOOSA, https://www.unoosa.org/oosa/en/ourwork/spacelaw/treaties/introliability-convention.html Accessed 25 November 2025.

58 UN DOC. A/AC.105/C.2/2025/CRP.9.

59 Art. VI of the Outer Space Treaty.

due to a fault on the part of another state, or indeed another hostile state, the former is entitled to compensation from the latter in accordance with the provisions of the Convention. This situation is clear and straightforward. However, some complex questions may arise regarding space objects involved in military activities in outer space.

Does a state have the right to claim compensation for damage caused to its national interests resulting from the collection and/or distribution of sensitive security data by another state using reconnaissance satellites and other techniques? The material scope of the Convention is limited to 'loss of life, personal injury or other impairment of health; or loss of life or damage to property of states or persons, natural or juridical, or property of international organisations'.[60] The type of loss covered by the Convention is physical. Therefore, any injury or damage to a state's interests, whether security, political, economic, or otherwise, would unquestionably fall outside the Convention's scope. Furthermore, damage caused by sharing sensitive data with third parties would not stem from the space object itself, but from actions taken by certain authorities after the reconnaissance mission is finished.[61]

Another question that arises in this context is: Can a state intentionally destroy a space object belonging to another state that poses a threat to the national security of the former without incurring any liability under the Convention? To answer this question, we must first determine whether the activity posing a threat to the national security of the other state was in conformity with international law. As will be seen later, many military space activities are not prohibited by international law. Therefore, any use of force against a space object engaged in such activity may amount to an act of aggression. It will trigger the application of the UN Charter provisions and, at the same time, attract liability under the Convention.

An analogous question is: Can a state use force against a space object engaged in any activity that is prohibited by international law in general and the Outer Space Treaty in particular? For instance, can a state disable a space object carrying weapons of mass destruction and possibly capture and confiscate it without attracting liability under the Convention? The Liability Convention, as well as the Outer Space Treaty, do not contain any enforcement mechanisms besides diplomatic consultations. According to the International Law Commission's 2001 draft Articles on State Responsibility for Internationally Wrongful Acts, countermeasures may be taken by a state in response to an internationally wrongful act by another state to procure cessation, provided that they are limited to non-forcible means.[62] Since the Outer Space Treaty's

60 Article I (a) of the Convention.

61 Gorove, *Studies in Space Law*, 126.

62 Commentary on Draft Article 1. United Nations, *Yearbook of the International Law Commission*, 2001, vol. II, Part Two, 32–4.

ban on stationing weapons of mass destruction in outer space benefits all states, any state would be entitled to undertake appropriate countermeasures to respond to such a breach. Non-forcible countermeasures could include intentional interference with communications systems, offensive cyber operations, or other non-forcible measures to disrupt, deny, disable, or delay the use or deployment of the weapons system.[63]

Another related question is whether a state is liable to pay compensation to another state for deliberately destroying its space object in the exercise of the right of self-defence? Article XXIII is clear on this point. Its first paragraph states:

> The provisions of this Convention shall not affect other international agreements in force in so far as relations between the States Parties to such agreements are concerned.

Therefore, in the situation described above, the UN Charter shall prevail. Consequently, there is no obligation to pay compensation if damage occurs while exercising a right granted by the UN Charter. Finally, one might question whether a state has the right to claim compensation under the Convention if a launching state intentionally causes harm to a person or property of the former on Earth's surface using a space weapon or any other device. Such damage falls outside the scope of the Convention. The Convention covers damage caused *by* a space object, not damage inflicted *from* a space object. Typically, the Convention addresses accidental damage, rather than intentional harm.

Situations like these are not merely hypothetical or science fiction, considering the serious plans by some countries to deploy anti-satellite and anti-ballistic missile weapons in outer space.[64] The issue of the applicability of international law concerning the use of force, particularly the Charter of the United Nations, to outer space is discussed later in this work. In conclusion, it may be observed that the Convention is not directly concerned with military activities in outer space. It does not aim to deter or compensate for nuclear war.[65] The provisions of the Convention are, practically speaking, mainly relevant to behaviour short of outright hostilities.[66] It establishes a regime to govern monetary compensation for losses incurred due to the negligent conduct of space activities or from the inherent risks associated with space activities.

63 Brian D. Green, 'Countering Space-Based Weapons of Mass Destruction', *Leiber Institute, West Point*, (31 January 2025). https://lieber.westpoint.edu/countering-space-based-weapons-mass-destruction-2/ Accessed 25 November 2025.

64 Current military activities in outer space are discussed in Chapter 3.

65 Ronald F. Stowe, 'The 1972 Convention on Liability for Damage Caused by Space Objects', in Nandasiri Jasentuliyana, ed., *Maintaining Outer Space for Peaceful Uses* (New York: United Nations University, 1984), 106.

66 Ibid.

The Registration Convention, 1975[67]

The Registration Convention was negotiated by the Legal Subcommittee of COPUOS from 1962 to 1974.[68] The General Assembly adopted it on 12 November 1974, opened for signature on 14 January 1975, and it entered into force on 125 November 1976.[69] As of 1 January 2025, it has 76 States Parties and three signatories. All the leading space powers are parties to it.

Identifying objects or vehicles in any international space open to all is essential for establishing and maintaining order in that environment. What can be said about airspace and the high seas is equally applicable to outer space. Registration of aircraft[70] and ships[71] is appropriately addressed by international law. The Outer Space Treaty mentions the registration of space objects but does not specify any procedures or modalities for it.[72] The Registration Convention outlines detailed rules for registering space objects, which are quite useful for their identification. It establishes a national register, an institutional register, and a United Nations register. While the procedures for national and institutional registration are left to the concerned states and institutions, provisions for registration with the UN are quite comprehensive. The UN Secretary-General is required to establish a register to record information furnished by States Parties in accordance with the Convention.[73] The information to be provided includes: Name of the launching state or states; an appropriate designator of the space object or its registration number; the date and territory or location of launch; basic orbital parameters including nodal period, inclination, apogee, and perigee; and the general function of the space object.[74]

It is not required for a space object to bear an identification mark or registration number. However, if a state opts to have one or both, it must notify the Secretary-General of the details.[75] Since identification is the key purpose of the Convention, the States Parties are expected to cooperate in identifying space objects that cause damage to other States or are hazardous

67 Full title: The Convention on Registration of Objects Launched into Outer Space, 1975. UN *Treaty Collection*, vol. 1023-I-15020.

68 UNOOSA, https://www.unoosa.org/oosa/en/ourwork/spacelaw/treaties/introregistration-convention.html Accessed 25 November 2025.

69 Ibid.

70 Articles 17, 18 and 19 of the Chicago Convention on International Civil Aviation, 1944. UN *Treaty Collection*, vol. 15-II-102.

71 Articles 4 to 7 of the United Nations Convention on the High Seas, 1958, UN *Treaty Collection*, vol. 450-I-6465; Articles 91 to 94 of the Law of the Sea Convention, 1982, UN *Treaty Collection*, vol. 1833-I-31363.

72 Article VIII.

73 Article III.

74 Article IV.

75 Article V.

or deleterious.[76] Those States Parties that have monitoring and tracking facilities are expected, 'to the greatest extent feasible', to respond to a request by a state party or the Secretary-General of the UN, under 'equitable and reasonable conditions in the identification of objects'.[77]

The Registration Convention and military activities

As noted earlier, the Convention does not specify the contents of the national register. It grants complete discretion to the States Parties to determine what information is to be recorded in such registers. Therefore, it is unreasonable to expect the States Parties to enter complete details of military space missions in their respective national registers. If national registration is intended for the convenience of States Parties, they have discretion to regulate its modalities. Overall, provisions concerning national registration lack practical significance.

Regarding the United Nations Register, it is unthinkable that states will be openly forthcoming in providing detailed disclosure about their space missions, especially those with military purposes. There appears to be little doubt that states will either avoid registering military space missions or provide insufficient or misleading information without explicitly indicating the mission's military nature. One of the significant difficulties is the suppression of material details in the interest of 'paramount considerations of national security'. It has been aptly noted that, with any limited information provided to the United Nations, it would be impossible to identify the precise nature of a space mission, and there may be a significant delay between the notification date and the launch.[78]

A review of the United Nations Office for Outer Space Affairs (UNOOSA) Index of Objects Launched into Outer Space shows that some states claim that their space objects' missions are 'Earth Observation' or 'Spacecraft engaged in practical applications and uses of space technology, such as weather or communications'.[79] These descriptions are too vague and unclear, and there is no assurance that the functions of these objects include reconnaissance. Very few states have stated that the purpose of their space objects is military communication.[80]

It is undeniable that registering space objects could greatly enhance peace and security in outer space. A well-structured, comprehensive, and informative register would prevent states from secretly deploying weapons of mass

76 Article VI.

77 Ibid.

78 Sune Danielson, 'International Security and Outer Space: Legal Aspects', *Disarmament*, X (1987), 114.

79 UNOOSA, https://www.unoosa.org/oosa/osoindex/search-ng.jspx?lf_id= Accessed 25 November 2025.

80 Ibid.

destruction in outer space.[81] An impractical suggestion to amend the Convention by inserting a new paragraph in Article IV was privately proposed in 1984:

> The State of registry shall immediately inform the Secretary-General of the United Nations in case any object carrying any kind of outer space weapons has been launched into outer space.[82]

It is unthinkable that space powers would ever agree to such an amendment. The Convention does not cover ballistic missiles, which traverse outer space but do not complete a full orbit. The Convention applies to space objects launched into Earth orbit or beyond.[83] The word 'launched' implies that the object is intended to remain in outer space for a significant period. It excludes objects expected to remain in outer space or Earth orbit for only a short time, such as a ballistic missile.

Overall, the Convention does not significantly support maintaining peace and security in outer space unless states actively involved in space activities choose to follow it both in letter and spirit, which seems unlikely, at least in the near future.

The Moon Treaty, 1979[84]

The Moon Treaty was negotiated from 1972 to 1979 and entered into force in 1984 after gaining its fifth ratification.[85] This treaty is not widely ratified. None of the leading space powers is a party to it. As of 1 January 2025, it has only 17 States Parties and four signatories.[86] The Treaty expands on the provisions of the Outer Space Treaty that apply to celestial bodies. Among other things, it declares that the moon and other celestial bodies shall be used exclusively for peaceful purposes and that their natural resources are the common heritage of mankind. It proposes the creation of an international regime governing the exploitation of celestial bodies' natural resources. Article 1 of the Treaty states that 'the provisions of this Agreement relating to the moon shall also apply to other celestial bodies within the solar system, other than the

81 I. H. Ph. Diederiks-Verschoor, 'Observations on the Registration Convention', in Nandasiri Jasentuliyana, ed., *Maintaining Outer Space for Peaceful Uses* (New York: United Nations University, 1984), 158–9.

82 He Quizi, 'The Registration Convention and Maintenance of the Peaceful Uses of Outer Space', in Nandasiri Jasentuliyana, ibid., 120.

83 Article II.

84 Full title: The Agreement Governing the Activities of States on the Moon and Other Celestial Bodies, 1979. UN *Treaty Collection*, vol. 1363-I-23002.

85 UNOOSA, https://www.unoosa.org/oosa/en/ourwork/spacelaw/treaties/intromoon-agreement.html Accessed 25 November 2025.

86 UN DOC. A/AC.105/C.2/2025/CRP.9.

Earth'. The Treaty guarantees freedom of scientific investigation on celestial bodies, protection of their natural environment, and allows the establishment of both manned and unmanned stations on them. Given the precarious nature of missions to celestial bodies, it also provides for assistance to persons in distress on them.[87]

The Moon Treaty and military activities

Article 3 of the Treaty comprehensively addresses military activities on celestial bodies. It reads as follows:

1. The moon shall be used by all States Parties exclusively for peaceful purposes.
2. Any threat or use of force or any other hostile act or threat of hostile act on the moon is prohibited. It is likewise prohibited to use the moon in order to commit any such act or to engage in any such threat in relation to the Earth, the moon, spacecraft, the personnel of spacecraft or man-made space objects.
3. States Parties shall not place in orbit around or other trajectory to or around the moon objects carrying nuclear weapons or any other kinds of weapons of mass destruction or place or use such weapons on or in the moon.
4. The establishment of military bases, installations and fortifications, the testing of any type of weapons and the conduct of military manoeuvres on the moon shall be forbidden. The use of military personnel for scientific research or for any other peaceful purposes shall not be prohibited. The use of any equipment or facility necessary for peaceful exploration and use of the moon shall also not be prohibited.

In many respects, this article resembles Article IV of the Outer Space Treaty. It further elaborates on the basic principles underlying Article IV. The first paragraph of Article 3 requires state parties to use celestial bodies exclusively for peaceful purposes. Despite the interpretative controversy surrounding the term 'peaceful purposes', it is qualified by the term 'exclusively', leaving no doubt that no military activity – whether aggressive or defensive-is permitted on celestial bodies. This is further clarified in the remaining paragraphs of Article 3.

The second paragraph of Article 3 resembles Article 2(4) of the UN Charter. Notably, the scope of Article 3(2) is considerably broader than that of Article 2(4) as it does not entitle States Parties to use force in a manner consistent

87 For an overview of the Treaty, see Bin Cheng, 'The Moon Treaty', *Current Legal Problems*, 33 (1980), 213–37.

with the purposes of the United Nations. It also forbids any hostile act or threat of hostile act on celestial bodies and from celestial bodies against the Earth, other celestial bodies, space objects, and their personnel. Does this imply that States Parties cannot exercise the right of self-defence on celestial bodies? France attached an explanation to the Treaty, stating that the provisions of Article 3(2) should not be construed as anything more than a reaffirmation of the prohibition on the use or threat of force in international relations as outlined in the United Nations Charter.[88]

The third paragraph of Article 3 prohibits placing nuclear or other weapons of mass destruction (a) in orbit around celestial bodies, (b) in a trajectory to or around celestial bodies, and (c) on or in celestial bodies. This extends the norm in Article IV of the Outer Space Treaty, which bans placing nuclear or other mass-destruction weapons in outer space and on celestial bodies. The final paragraph of Article 3 is an *ad verbatim* copy of the second sentence of the second paragraph of Article IV of the Outer Space Treaty, which forbids the establishment of military bases, installations, fortifications, weapons testing, military manoeuvres, and similar activities on celestial bodies. It further reinforces the argument that celestial bodies have been completely demilitarised. However, in one respect, Article 3(4) differs from Article IV of the Outer Space Treaty. This difference arises from the unique definition of the moon in Article 1(2) of the Treaty. This paragraph states:

> For the purposes of this Agreement reference to the moon shall include orbits around or other trajectories to or around it.

Orbits around or other trajectories to or from celestial bodies are part of outer space proper. As observed earlier, apart from deploying nuclear or other weapons of mass destruction, other military activities are not prohibited in outer space. However, under Article 1(2) and other provisions of this article, orbits around celestial bodies and trajectories to or around them are fully demilitarised.

Article 15 of the Treaty may indirectly promote the demilitarisation of celestial bodies. It grants a right to the States Parties to visit facilities of other States Parties on celestial bodies to verify whether their activities comply with the treaty. However, such visits are subject to reasonable notice and must involve taking maximum precautions to ensure safety and avoid undue interference. These visits are not required to be reciprocal, unlike the arrangement under the Outer Space Treaty.[89] While such visits need to be preplanned, in cases of disagreement or deadlock in planning, the possibility of unilateral recourse to the United Nations Secretary-General for resolution is provided.

88 See depository notification, UN *Treaty Collection*, vol. 1363-I-56487.

89 Article XII of the Outer Space Treaty.

Nonetheless, it remains uncertain how effectively this provision will ensure a State Party's right to access facilities of other states on celestial bodies. Beyond good faith consultations, no additional obligations exist for the parties, even if they possess space vehicles, equipment, facilities, stations, or installations on celestial bodies. Overall, such visits appear unlikely given the technological capabilities needed to execute them.

From the language of Article 3(3), some writers are tempted to infer that weapons other than nuclear or mass-destruction weapons may be placed on or used in celestial bodies.[90] However, given the rest of the provisions of Article 3 that unequivocally demilitarise celestial bodies, placing any weapons on them is forbidden. The placement of weapons other than nuclear or mass-destruction weapons in orbits around celestial bodies or in a trajectory to or around them is not explicitly prohibited. Nonetheless, due to the unusual definition of celestial bodies in Article 1(2), as previously noted, it can be suggested that they are also demilitarised. Another suggestion is that certain weapons might be deployed on celestial bodies for deterrence to maintain international peace and security, since such deployment could be considered the use of celestial bodies for 'peaceful purposes'.[91] The United States' official position, as expressed in a statement by a Department of Defence official during a congressional hearing on the Moon Treaty ratification, is similar.

> We will be looking carefully at the language of the treaty, and in particular Article 3 . . . to insure that certain possible non-aggressive military activities in deep-space or in the vicinity of the moon are not precluded. In this regard, we will want to insure that the treaty's reference to peaceful purposes and to the threat or use of force are interpreted in a manner consistent with US interpretation of the Outer Space Treaty and the United Nations Charter.[92]

The United States delegate to the COPUOS had, immediately after adopting the text of the treaty, made it clear that the United States would continue to interpret 'peaceful' as 'non-aggressive'.[93] Be that as it may, the word 'peaceful' in Article 3 is qualified by the word 'exclusively'. A specific reference to the use of celestial bodies for 'exclusively peaceful' purposes rules out even non-aggressive activities, and it means that the celestial bodies must not be

90 See generally, N. M. Matte, 'Legal Principles Relating to the Moon', *Annals of Air and Space Law*, 3 (1978), 511–44.

91 D. Goedhuis, 'Some Recent Trends in the Interpretation and Implementation of the Rules of International Space Law', *Columbia Journal of Transnational Law*, 19 (1981), 227.

92 U.S. Senate, 96th Congress, 'Statement of Assistant Secretary of Defence for International Security Affairs in Hearings Before the Sub-Committee on Science and Technology and Space, of the Committee on Commerce, Science and Technology', (July 1980), 145–7.

93 U.N. Doc. A/AC.105/PV.203, 22.

used for any military activity – defensive, non-aggressive, or offensive. In the context of celestial bodies, 'peaceful' means non-military.[94]

Although the Moon Treaty is a remarkable instrument, as previously mentioned, the major space-faring nations have opted not to participate in it. Some States Parties have even decided to withdraw; on 5 January 2023, Saudi Arabia notified the UN Secretary-General of its withdrawal from the Treaty.[95] It is believed that the United States and the Soviet Union were not genuinely committed to establishing a treaty governing celestial bodies. Nonetheless, they agreed to negotiate to keep the COPUOS occupied with the treaty process, so as not to hinder their space activities.[96]

The United States has initiated the development of principles for the safe exploration of the moon and other celestial bodies, as well as outer space, through the Artemis Accords, founded in 2020, outside the framework of the COPUOS. They are a set of statements that outline common principles, guidelines, and best practices applicable to the safe exploration of the moon and other celestial bodies.[97] Co-led by the National Aeronautics and Space Administration (NASA) and the United States Department of State, these accords are voluntarily signed at a national level. So far, they do not appear to affect military activities on celestial bodies.[98] Saudi Arabia's withdrawal from the Moon Treaty immediately after signing the Artemis Accord does not seem to be a mere coincidence. It is no wonder that other States Parties to the Moon Treaty might also follow suit if they are tempted to sign the Artemis Accords. In response to the Artemis Accords, China and Russia intend to establish an International Lunar Research Centre and construct a nuclear power plant to supply it with energy.[99]

Concluding remarks

In conclusion, it is essential to highlight that the Outer Space Treaty and the Moon Treaty contain specific provisions concerning military activities in outer space. While the Moon Treaty is not widely ratified, it can be argued,

94 Cheng, 'Properly Speaking', 107.

95 Stefan-Michael Wedenig and Jack Wright Nelson, 'The Moon Agreement: Hanging by a Thread?', *McGill Institute of Air and Space Law*, (26 January 2023). https://www.mcgill.ca/iasl/article/moon-agreement-hanging-thread Accessed 25 November 2025.

96 Ibid.

97 Robert Lee, 'Artemis Accords: What Are They and Which Countries are Involved?', *Space.Com*, (9 April 2025). https://www.space.com/artemis-accords-explained Accessed 25 November 2025.

98 Ibid.

99 Eduardo Baptista, 'China, Russia May Build Nuclear Plant on Moon to Power Lunar Station, Official Says', *Reuters*, (23 April 2025). https://www.reuters.com/business/energy/china-led-lunar-base-include-nuclear-power-plant-moons-surface-space-official-2025-04-23/ Accessed 25 November 2025.

based on consistent and extensive state practice since the early days of space exploration, that the obligation to use celestial bodies solely for peaceful purposes and the norm that they have been entirely demilitarised have become part of customary international law. The recent trend to bypass the Moon Treaty through national initiatives such as the Artemis Accords focuses more on the resources of celestial bodies than on their demilitarisation. Therefore, the combined effect of these treaties is that celestial bodies are completely demilitarised, banning any military activity on or in them – offensive or defensive, aggressive or non-aggressive – even if we interpret 'peaceful' as 'non-aggressive'. Conversely, outer space, excluding celestial bodies, has been partially de-weaponised. The stationing of nuclear or other weapons of mass destruction in outer space is explicitly forbidden. Therefore, outer space remains accessible for other military activities. Additionally, other space treaties indirectly address certain aspects of military operations in outer space, primarily focusing on three issues: The rescue and return of astronauts and space objects, liability for damages caused by space objects, and the registration of space objects. The cooperative spirit that led to the adoption of five space treaties within 12 years no longer exists due to the political, scientific, and technological changes that have occurred since then.

References

Baptista E., 'China, Russia May Build Nuclear Plant on Moon to Power Lunar Station, Official Says', *Reuters*, (23 April 2025). https://www.reuters.com/business/energy/china-led-lunar-base-include-nuclear-power-plant-moons-surface-space-official-2025-04-23/ Accessed 25 November 2025.

Bhardwaj T. and Joshi T., 'Analyzing the Obligation to Recover and Return Space Objects Upon Controlled Re-Entry Under International Space Law', *Paper Presented at the 74th International Astronautical Congress, Baku, Azerbaijan*, (2–6 October 2023), 7. https://iafastro.directory/iac/archive/browse/IAC-23/E7/1/77008/ Accessed 25 November 2025.

Caves J. P., Jr. and Carus W. S., *The Future of Weapons of Mass Destruction: Their Nature and Role in 2030*. Washington, DC: National Defence University, 2014.

Cheng B., 'The 1968 Astronauts Agreement or How Not to Make a Treaty', *Yearbook of World Affairs*, 23 (1969), 185–208.

Cheng B., 'Le Traite de 1967 sur l'espace', (English Translation) *Journal du Droit International*, 95 (1968), 534–44.

Cheng B., 'The Legal Status of Outer Space and Relevant Issues: Delimitation of Outer Space and Definition of Peaceful Use', *Journal of Space Law*, 11 (1983), 89–105.

Cheng B., 'The Moon Treaty', *Current Legal Problems*, 33 (1980), 213–37.

Cheng B., 'Outer Space: The International Legal Framework', *Thesaurus Acroasium*, X (1981), 66–72.

Cheng B., 'Properly Speaking, Only Celestial Bodies Have Been Reserved for Use Exclusively for Peaceful (Non-Military) Purpose, But Not Outer Void Space', *International Law Studies*, 75 (2000), 81–117.

Danielson S., 'International Security and Outer Space: Legal Aspects', *Disarmament*, X (1987), 107–27.

Dembling P. G. and Arons D. M., 'Space Law and the United Nations: The Work of the Legal Subcommittee of the United Nations Committee on the Peaceful Uses of Outer Space', *Journal of Air Law and Commerce*, 32 (1966), 329–86.

Diederiks-Verschoor I. P. S., 'Observations on the Registration Convention', in Jasentuliyana N., ed., *Maintaining Outer Space for Peaceful Uses*. New York: United Nations University, 1984, 157–62.

Fawcett J. E. S., *Outer Space: New Challenges to Law and Policy*. Oxford: Oxford University Press, 1984.

Goedhuis D., 'Some Recent Trends in the Interpretation and Implementation of the Rules of International Space Law', *Columbia Journal of Transnational Law*, 19 (1981), 213–33.

Gorove S., 'Arms Control Provisions in the Outer Space Treaty: A Scrutinizing Reappraisal', *Georgia Journal of International and Comparative Law*, 3 (1973), 114–23.

Gorove S., *Studies in Space Law: Its Challenges and Prospects*. Leiden: A.W. Sijthoff, 1977.

Green B. D., 'Countering Space-Based Weapons of Mass Destruction', *Leiber Institute, West Point*, (31 January 2025). https://lieber.westpoint.edu/countering-space-based-weapons-mass-destruction-2/ Accessed 25 November 2025.

Hearsay C., 'Comparative Study on the Definition of Space Object in National Space Laws and Its Legal Effect Under International Law', *Social Science Research Network*, (May 2012). https://ssrn.com/abstract=2072514 Accessed 25 November 2025.

Horowitz M. C. and Narang N., 'Poor Man's Atomic Bomb? Exploring the Relationship Between "Weapons of Mass Destruction"', *Journal of Conflict Resolution*, 58 (2014), 509–35.

Jaksetic E., 'The Peaceful Uses of Outer Space: Soviet Views', *American University Law Review*, 28 (1979), 483–506.

Lachs M., *The Law of Outer Space: An Experience in Contemporary Law Making*. Leiden: A.W. Sijthoff, 1972.

Lee R., 'Artemis Accords: What are They and Which Countries are Involved?', *Space.Com*, (9 April 2025). https://www.space.com/artemis-accords-explained Accessed 25 November 2025.

Matte N. M., *Aerospace Law*. Toronto: Sweet & Maxwell Ltd., 1969.

Matte N. M., 'Legal Principles Relating to the Moon', *Annals of Air and Space Law*, 3 (1978), 511–44.

Maxwell P. B., *Interpretation of Statutes*. Bombay: N.M. Tripathi & Co., 1968.

McMahon J. F., 'Legal Aspects of Outer Space', *British Yearbook of International Law*, 38 (1962), 339–61.

McNair A. D., *The Law of Treaties*. Oxford: Oxford University Press, 1961.

Muskat M., 'New Developments in Outer Space and Their Role in Increasing International Security', *Zeitschrift Fur Auslandisches Offentliches Recht und Volkerrecht*, 30 (1970), 113–24.

Quizi H., 'The Registration Convention and Maintenance of the Peaceful Uses of Outer Space', in Jasentuliyana N., ed., *Maintaining Outer Space for Peaceful Uses*. New York: United Nations University, 1984, 117–20.

Reed W. D. and Norris R. W., 'Military Uses of the Space Shuttle', *Akron Law Review*, 13 (1980), 665–88.

Scharf M., 'Accelerated Formation of Customary International Law', *ILSA Journal of International and Comparative Law*, 20 (2013–14), 324–8.

Stowe R. F., 'The 1972 Convention on Liability for Damage Caused by Space Objects', in Jasentuliyana N., ed., *Maintaining Outer Space for Peaceful Uses*. New York: United Nations University, 1984, 95–124.

Tatsuzawa K., 'Some Observations on the Meaning of the Term "Peaceful Uses" in Space Law', *Proceedings of the Thirtieth Colloquium on the Law of Outer Space*, (1987), 44–8.

Thomsen D., 'Strategic Defense of X-Ray Initiative', *The Free Library*, (14 December 1985). http://www.thefreelibrary.com/Strategic+defense+of+X-ray+initiative.-a04060251 Accessed 25 November 2025.

UN Doc. A/AC.105/C.2/2025/CRP.9.

UN Doc. A/AC.105/C.2/L.1.

UN Doc. A/AC 105/C.2/L.2/Rev. 1.

UN Doc. A/AC.105/C.2/SR 65.

UN Doc. A/AC.105/C.2/SR.76.

UN Doc. A/AC.105/C.2/SR.86.

UN Doc. A/AC.105/PV.49.

UN Doc. A/AC.105/PV.203.

UN *Treaty Collection*, vol. 15-II-102.

UN *Treaty Collection*, vol. 402-I-5778.

UN *Treaty Collection*, vol. 450-I-6465.

UN *Treaty Collection*, vol. 672-I-9574.

UN *Treaty Collection*, vol. 961-I-13810.

UN *Treaty Collection*, vol. 1023-I-15020.

UN *Treaty Collection*, vol. 1363-I-23002.

UN *Treaty Collection*, vol. 1363-I-56487.

UN *Treaty Collection*, vol. 1833-I-31363.

UN *Treaty Collection*, vol. 3370-I-56478.

UNGA Res. 172A (XIV), 12 December 1959.

UNGA Res. 1348 (XIII), 13 December 1958.

UNGA Res. 1721A (XVI), 20 December 1961.

UNGA Res. 1962 (XVIII), 13 December 1962.

United Nations, *Yearbook of the International Law Commission*, 2001, vol. II, Part Two.

UNOOSA, https://www.unoosa.org/oosa/en/ourwork/copuos/index.html Accessed 25 November 2025.

UNOOSA, https://www.unoosa.org/oosa/en/ourwork/spacelaw/treaties/introliability-convention.html Accessed 25 November 2025.

UNOOSA, https://www.unoosa.org/oosa/en/ourwork/spacelaw/treaties/intromoon-agreement.html Accessed 25 November 2025.

UNOOSA, https://www.unoosa.org/oosa/en/ourwork/spacelaw/treaties/introregistration-convention.html Accessed 25 November 2025.

UNOOSA, https://www.unoosa.org/oosa/osoindex/search-ng.jspx?lf_id= Accessed 25 November 2025.

U.S. Department of State, 'Declassification and Release of the Confidential Document: Definition of Peaceful Uses of Outer Space'. https://www.

cia.gov/readingroom/docs/CIA-RDP66R00638R000100160004-2.pdf Accessed 25 November 2025.

U.S. Senate, 96th Congress, 'Statement of Assistant Secretary of Defence for International Security Affairs in Hearings before the Sub-Committee on Science and Technology and Space, of the Committee on Commerce, Science and Technology', (July 1980), 145–7.

Wadegaonkar D., *The Orbit of Space Law*. Bombay: N.M. Tripathi & Co., 1984.

Wedenig S. and Nelson J. W., 'The Moon Agreement: Hanging by a Thread?', *McGill Institute of Air and Space Law*, (26 January 2023). https://www.mcgill.ca/iasl/article/moon-agreement-hanging-thread Accessed 25 November 2025.

Zedalis R. and Wade C., 'Anti-Satellite Weapons and Outer Space Treaty of 1967', *California Western International Law Journal*, 8 (1978), 454–66.

Zukov G. P., 'On the Question of Interpretation of the Term "Peaceful Uses of Outer Space" Contained in the Space Treaty', *Proceedings of the Eleventh Colloquium on the Law of Outer Space*, (1968).

2 General international law and military activities in outer space

The rules governing the resort to force form a fundamental part of public international law and are essential for maintaining international peace and security. Confrontation and conflict between states can occur on land, at sea, in airspace, and in outer space. These rules are therefore key to governing military operations in outer space. Besides these rules, certain other aspects of international law also have some implications for military activities in outer space. These are discussed in this chapter. However, the first and most crucial question to address is: Whether international law applies to outer space?

Applicability of international law to outer space activities

Since the beginning of the space age, there has never been any doubt that human activities in outer space are governed by international law. There was never a legal vacuum in outer space. This was confirmed in 1961 when the United Nations General Assembly adopted a resolution promoting international cooperation in the peaceful uses of outer space, explicitly stating that international law, including the Charter of the United Nations, applies to outer space and celestial bodies.[1] This was followed by the Declaration of Legal Principles resolution adopted in 1963, which also stipulates that 'the activities of States in the exploration and use of outer space shall be conducted in accordance with international law, including the Charter of the United Nations, to maintain international peace and security and foster international co-operation and understanding'.[2] This was reiterated in most resolutions of the UN General Assembly on outer space, as well as in the preambles of all space treaties adopted so far. These statements have a declaratory character rather than establishing a new rule of international law that defines its scope.[3]

1 UNGA Res. 1721 (XVI).

2 UNGA Res. 1962 (XVIII).

3 Bin Cheng, 'The Extraterrestrial Application of International Law', *Current Legal Problems*, 18 (1965), 151; Guyala Gal, *Space Law* (Leiden: A.W. Sijthoff, 1969), 131 and Lachs, *The Law of Outer Space*, 109.

DOI: 10.4324/9781003754428-3

Regarding the scope of international law's application to outer space activities, Bin Cheng has conducted a detailed analysis of the extraterrestrial nature of international law, particularly relating to the concept of jurisdiction. He states:

> As a result of man's penetration into space, all the rules of international law governing the attribution and exercise of quasi-territorial and personal jurisdiction become fully applicable extra-terrestrially whenever spacecraft and nationals of members of the international society venture beyond the territorial airspace.[4]

Certain areas of international law are more pertinent than others for extraterrestrial application. They, along with specific norms developed for application in outer space, constitute the entire corpus of international legal norms applicable to outer space. It is also possible that some norms of general international law are modified by special norms developed in the context of outer space activities.

While declaring that international law applies to outer space and celestial bodies, the resolutions of the General Assembly, as well as the space treaties adopted to date, specifically affirm that the United Nations Charter also applies to outer space.

Use of force and self-defence in and from outer space

Since the early days of international law, the issue of the use of force has often been a potential source of disagreement.[5] Over the centuries, the law governing the use of force has developed to specify the circumstances in which military force may be legitimately used. The United Nations Charter, adopted just after the Second World War, prohibits the use of force in international relations to 'save the succeeding generations from the scourge of war' unless such force aligns with the United Nations' purposes. Consequently, Article 2(4) of the Charter states:

> All Members shall refrain in their international relations from the threat or use of force against the territorial integrity or political independence of any state, or in any other manner inconsistent with the Purposes of the United Nations.

This provision has attained the status of customary law, binding all states regardless of their membership in the United Nations.[6]

4 Ibid., 132–52.

5 See generally, Ian Brownlie, *International Law and Use of Force by States* (Oxford: Oxford University Press, 1968).

6 *Military and Paramilitary Activities in and against Nicaragua Case (Nicaragua v. United States)* (Merits) I.C.J. Reports, 1986, 97–8. http://www.icj-cij.org/docket/files/70/6503.pdf Accessed 25 November 2025.

Article 42 of the Charter authorises collective forcible action with the Security Council's authorisation to maintain international peace and security. Additionally, Article 51 affirms the inherent right of individual and collective self-defence in response to an armed attack against a United Nations member, subject to specific conditions. These are the only two explicitly stated scenarios in the Charter in which a state may use military force against another, either individually or collectively. The debate continues over whether a state can use military force to halt severe human rights violations in another country on humanitarian grounds. Even more contentious is the concept of 'Responsibility to Protect', which seemingly permits a state to use force against another to protect its civilians. Moreover, recent major conflicts such as those in the Democratic Republic of Congo, Syria, Sudan, Ukraine-Russia, Israel-Hamas-Hezbollah, and Israel-Iran have placed a significant strain on the law governing the use of force. In the early years of the United Nations, the Charter's collective security principles failed to maintain peace and security, primarily due to Cold War rivalries and, after the Cold War, because of the multipolar distribution of power among key member states, particularly the permanent members of the Security Council.

Today, outer space is widely used by many states for various essential services. Any deliberate interference with or attack on a space object providing these services could have disastrous consequences for the affected state's security. As will be discussed in the next chapter, the process of militarising outer space, especially its weaponisation, is being seriously pursued by some states. Outer space is seen as a future battleground. Any conflict between states in outer space will inevitably lead to a confrontation on Earth, and vice versa. Considering this, the concepts of 'use of force' and 'self-defence' require a conscious re-examination in the context of outer space.

Article 2(4) of the United Nations Charter applies to all situations of armed confrontation in outer space or involving outer space. The phrase 'use of force against political independence or territorial integrity' is broad enough to include the use of force against objects in outer space and on celestial bodies, as well as force from objects in outer space or on celestial bodies against objects in outer space, on celestial bodies, airspace, the high seas, and terrestrial Earth. The phrase 'political independence or territorial integrity' encompasses the total of legal rights a state possesses.[7] Any violation of Article 2(4) amounting to an armed attack authorises the victim state to invoke Article 51 of the Charter and use force in self-defence.[8]

Another related question is whether the use of force by a state against another state's space assets would constitute an act of aggression. The definition

7 See generally, Chapter XIII, Brownlie, *International Law and Use of Force*.

8 Only 'most grave form of use of force' amounts to an armed attack according to the I.C.J. decision in *Nicaragua v. United States*, *I.C.J. Reports*, 1986, 101.

of aggression, adopted unanimously by the General Assembly in 1974, is regarded as authoritative.[9] Article 1 of this definition states:

> Aggression is the use of armed force by a State against the sovereignty, territorial integrity or political independence of another State, or in any other manner inconsistent with the Charter of the United Nations, as set out in this Definition.[10]

Article 39 of the Charter, which uses the term 'aggression', focuses on determining who is responsible for violating the UN Charter's prohibition on the use of force. This is essential to invoke the Security Council's authority to take measures to maintain international peace and security, as outlined in Articles 41 and 42. An act of aggression involves a serious, direct or indirect use of force amounting to an armed attack, as exemplified by the consensus definition. Such an act also triggers the application of Article 51 of the Charter, which affirms the inherent right of self-defence. A state may initiate an armed attack in self-defence, but an act of aggression can never be justified as self-defence. According to Article 2 of the definition, the first use of armed force by a state would constitute an act of aggression unless the Security Council determines otherwise in the circumstances. Aggression is an international crime under the Rome Statute of the International Criminal Court.[11] Not every use of force constitutes an armed attack. It must possess a certain level of gravity to be considered an armed attack.[12] The International Court of Justice has also endorsed this view by noting that only 'the most grave forms of use of force' qualify as an armed attack.[13] However, the Court did not specify the threshold of gravity required to qualify as an armed attack. The decision in The Oil Platforms case observed that the threshold is adaptable and varies according to the circumstances of each case.[14]

Article 3 of the 1974 definition outlines specific acts that may constitute aggression. Clause (d) states:

> An attack by the armed forces of a State on the land, sea or air forces, or marine and air fleets of another State;

Although this clause does not explicitly refer to military space objects, the analogy is quite pertinent. Article 1 of the definition is sufficiently broad to include attacks on civilian space objects. Furthermore, the list of acts in Article 3 is only

9 UN General Assembly Resolution 3314 (XXIX), 14 December 1974.
10 Ibid.
11 Article 8 *bis* of the Statute. UN *Treaty Collection*, vol. 2187-I-38544.
12 Brownlie, *International Law and the Use of Force*, 366.
13 *Nicaragua v. United States*, (Merits) 1986, para 191, and *Oil Platforms Case (Iran v. United States)*, 2003, para 51. http://www.icj-cij.org/docket/files/90/9715.pdf Accessed 25 November 2025.
14 *Iran v. United States, ICJ Rep* 161, para 72.

illustrative, not exhaustive. The definition of the crime of aggression in Article 8 *bis* of the Rome Statute of the International Criminal Court follows the framework and language of the General Assembly's definition.[15] An aggressive act in outer space might qualify as an armed attack under Article 2(4) of the United Nations Charter, enabling the targeted state to exercise the right of self-defence both in outer space and on Earth's surface. This could potentially lead to a situation of international armed conflict, as defined by international law, particularly international humanitarian law.

Although the right of self-defence is well-established in customary international law and explicitly outlined in the United Nations Charter, its precise scope and content remain subject to debate. Brownlie argues that the right of self-defence as it exists today has evolved through legal developments since the time of the League of Nations.[16] During the period from 1920 to 1939, states began discarding war or the use of force as instruments of national policy, leading to the refinement of the classical right of self-preservation. The residual right that remained to justify actions necessary solely for maintaining the integrity of the territorial domain is the right of self-defence.[17] Bowett disagrees and argues that Article 51 does not prevent states from resorting to the customary right of self-defence, which is much broader than Article 51.[18] He asserts that members of the United Nations possess all the rights granted to them by general international law, unless and to the extent that they have relinquished those rights under the Charter.[19] It is widely acknowledged that the traditional right of self-defence permits anticipatory or preventive forcible measures in response to an imminent armed attack. The renowned *Caroline* formula would allow states to take anticipatory forcible measures if there is '. . . a necessity of self-defence, instant, overwhelming, leaving no choice of means and no moment for deliberation'.[20] Brownlie believes that this formula is now outdated due to several changes that have occurred between 1920 and 1939.[21] A major difficulty with anticipatory self-defence is that it involves assessing the likelihood of an attack, which requires understanding a government's intentions, potentially leading to serious conflict if the situation is misunderstood.[22] Since

15 UN *Treaty Collection*, vol. 2187-I-38544.

16 Brownlie, *International Law and the Use of Force*, 274.

17 Ibid., 251–2.

18 D. W. Bowett, *Self-defence in International Law* (New York: Praeger, 1958), 185.

19 Ibid.

20 Lawfulness of the British seizure of the American ship Caroline during the Canadian rebellion of 1837 was discussed in correspondence between the United States and British officials. The *Caroline* formula is a part of this correspondence. For the text, see D. J. Harris, *Cases and Materials on International Law* (London: Sweet & Maxwell, 1983), 655–6.

21 Ian Brownlie, 'The Maintenance of Peace and Security in Outer Space', *British Yearbook of International Law*, 40 (1964), 21.

22 Brownlie, *International Law and Use of Force*, 259.

the law concerning the use of force and self-defence extends to outer space and celestial bodies, this matter is further discussed in Chapter 4.

Application of international humanitarian law to armed conflict in outer space

International humanitarian law comprises a set of norms and rules aimed at reducing the humanitarian impact of armed conflicts by limiting the means and methods of warfare that parties to a conflict can use and ensuring the protection and humane treatment of individuals who are not, or are no longer, directly participating in hostilities.[23]

This law – *jus in bello* – applies to all instances involving military force, regardless of whether such force is deemed legal or illegal under international law concerning the use of force – *jus ad bellum.* The traditional concept of 'Law of War' has now been replaced by 'international humanitarian law' due to the humanitarian considerations that motivated the modern development of this law and its basis in the principle of humanity. Since the mid-twentieth century, the term 'war' has been substituted by 'armed conflict' in all legal discourse within international humanitarian law. In international law, war is primarily a political concept rather than a factual one. In traditional international law, a state of war did not exist until a declaration of war was issued. Today, the broader concept of armed conflict is no longer dependent on a formal declaration of war. Because,

> [t]he notion of 'international armed conflict' is much broader than the traditional concept of 'war'. It includes (i) the use of force in a warlike manner between states, whether they recognize themselves at being war or not; (ii) all 'measures short of war', whether they are comparable with Article 2 (4) of the U.N. Charter or not; and (iii) wars of national liberation.[24]

International humanitarian law also applies to non-international armed conflicts. The Rome Statute of the International Criminal Court defines non-international armed conflict as:

> armed conflicts that take place in the territory of a State when there is protracted armed conflict between governmental authorities and organised armed groups or between such groups.[25]

23 Nils Melzer, *International Humanitarian Law: A Comprehensive Introduction* (Geneva: ICRC, 2016), 17.

24 *Max Planck Encyclopaedias of Public International Law*, vol. 7 (Oxford: Oxford University Press, 1985), 26.

25 Article 8 (2)(f) of the Statute.

Some states that might sympathise with the cause of a non-state armed group could permit such groups to utilise their space infrastructure to conduct hostilities against their adversaries. Additionally, a state may conduct hostilities from outer space against targets belonging to organised armed groups on the Earth's surface. Therefore, international humanitarian law may be relevant to hostilities in non-international armed conflicts involving outer space.

As will be seen in the next chapter, today, outer space is being used for specific military purposes, and plans to use it for additional military applications, including the development and deployment of space weapon systems, are actively pursued. Considering this, it is possible to envisage different scenarios of armed hostilities using outer space:

1. From land territory, airspace, coastal waters, or the high seas against targets in outer space or on celestial bodies.
2. From outer space against targets in outer space itself or on celestial bodies.
3. From outer space against targets on the surface of the Earth, the seas, and the airspace.
4. From a celestial body against targets on the same or another celestial body.
5. From a celestial body against targets in outer space.
6. From a celestial body against targets on the surface of the Earth, the seas, and the airspace.

As of today, the use of force from celestial bodies seems unlikely. It might become possible in the coming decades. Although the Outer Space Treaty and the Moon Treaty have completely demilitarised celestial bodies, without an effective verification mechanism, it remains uncertain whether the Treaty rules will be fully respected in good faith. Furthermore, the Moon Treaty has very few signatories, and none of the major space powers are party to it.

The six situations outlined previously clearly have implications for international humanitarian law. These scenarios might arise during an existing terrestrial international armed conflict between the concerned states. The use of force by a state against an opponent's space infrastructure could trigger an armed conflict even if there are no terrestrial hostilities between those states. It is recognised that an armed conflict exists whenever armed force is employed between two or more states.[26] Applying this test shows that using force from or in outer space will likely lead to armed conflict, thereby triggering the application of international humanitarian law. The International Committee of the Red Cross has consistently maintained that military operations

26 *Prosecutor v. Dusko Tadic aka "Dule" (Decision on the Defence Motion for Interlocutory Appeal on Jurisdiction)*, IT-94-1, International Criminal Tribunal for the Former Yugoslavia (ICTY), 2 October 1995. https://www.refworld.org/jurisprudence/caselaw/icty/1995/en/61438 para 70 Accessed 25 November 2025.

in outer space, or related to it, are constrained by international humanitarian law.[27] Nevertheless, those closely monitoring the militarisation of outer space strongly advocate for further development of humanitarian law, primarily to address potential armed confrontations in outer space, given the unprecedented challenges that space warfare might present.[28]

Some multilateral treaty obligations

Certain multilateral treaties, although not explicitly adopted for outer space, contain provisions that impose legal obligations on States Parties relevant to some of their outer space activities. Such treaties can be regarded as complementary instruments for securing order in outer space. From this perspective, examining a few multilateral treaties is desirable for this work.

The first is the Treaty Banning Nuclear Weapon Tests in the Atmosphere, in Outer Space and Under Water, adopted on 5 August 1963 at Moscow and coming into force on 10 October 1963, commonly known as the Limited or Partial Test Ban Treaty (LTBT/PTBT).[29] This was followed by the Comprehensive Test Ban Treaty (CTBT) in 1996, which was expected to replace the PTBT. However, the CTBT has not come into force due to the non-ratification by the states whose ratification is a prerequisite for it to enter into force. The major space powers, except China and France, were parties to the PTBT, but in November 2023, Russia withdrew from the treaty.[30] The primary concern of this treaty, as stated in its preamble, is 'the discontinuance of all test explosions of nuclear weapons for all time', and 'putting an end to the contamination of man's environment by radioactive substances'. The focus is on safeguarding the environment from radioactive contamination rather than arms control. Nevertheless, testing of nuclear weapons in outer space – one of the most insidious military activities – is categorically prohibited by the treaty. This is a notable achievement of the treaty.

The second relevant treaty is the Convention on the Prohibition of Military or any other Hostile Use of Environmental Modification Techniques of 1976 (ENMOD Convention). It bans States Parties from using environmental modification techniques for military or hostile purposes that have widespread, long-lasting, or severe effects as a method of destruction, damage, or injury to

27 ICRC, 'Outer Space Weapons and International Humanitarian Law'. https://www.icrc.org/en/law-and-policy/weapons-outer-space Accessed 25 November 2025.

28 Fabio van Loon, 'Codifying *Jus in Bello Spatialis*: The Space Law of Tomorrow', *Strategic Studies Quarterly*, 15 (2021), 15.

29 UN *Treaty Collection*, vol. 480-I-6964.

30 Arms Control Association, 'Russia Withdraws Ratification of Nuclear Test Ban Treaty', (2 November 2023). https://www.armscontrol.org/blog/2023-11/nuclear-disarmament-monitor Accessed 25 November 2025.

any other State Party.[31] The Convention defines 'environmental modification techniques' as 'any techniques for changing through the deliberate manipulation of natural processes the dynamics, composition, or structure of the Earth, including its biota, lithosphere, hydrosphere, and atmosphere, or of *outer space*'.[32]

The Treaty on the Prohibition of Nuclear Weapons, adopted in 2017, has not been signed or ratified by any nuclear power.[33] As of May 2025, it has 94 signatories and 73 States Parties – almost all of which are from developing countries and non-nuclear-weapon states. It entered into force in January 2021. Although major nuclear powers – including space-faring nations – are unlikely to accede to the Treaty in the foreseeable future, it is important to note that the Treaty reinforces the Outer Space Treaty's prohibition on placing nuclear weapons or weapons of mass destruction in outer space and on celestial bodies.

Effect of outbreak of hostilities on space treaties

One pertinent issue that must be considered in the present context is: What would be the effect of the outbreak of hostilities between parties to the space treaties on such treaties? Upon the outbreak of war and hostilities, some treaty obligations are abrogated, some are suspended, and others continue to bind the States Parties, irrespective of the existence of a state of war. The growing reliance on treaties to govern activities in outer space requires further examination.

The Vienna Convention on the Law of Treaties of 1969 does not address the impact of hostilities on treaty obligations. Thus, Article 73 states:

> The provisions of the present convention shall not prejudge any question that may arise in regard to a treaty . . . from the outbreak of hostilities between states.

This requires a reference to customary law. The primary requirement under customary law for determining the effect of hostilities on a treaty is to identify the nature and type of the treaty. To this end, customary law categorises treaties in various kinds.[34] One of these is multipartite law-making treaties. Outer space treaties examined in Chapter 1 are undoubtedly multipartite law-making treaties. Regarding such treaties, McNair concludes that they are unaffected

31 Article I of the Convention. For full text, see UN *Treaty Collection*, vol. 1108-I-17119.

32 Article II, ibid. Emphasis added.

33 Status of the Treaty as of 3 June 2025. https://treaties.un.org/pages/viewdetails.aspx?src=treaty&mtdsg_no=xxvi-9&chapter=26&clang=_en Accessed 25 November 2025.

34 McNair, *The Law of Treaties*, 703–27.

by the outbreak of war between all or only some of the parties.[35] The decisive point is that the states participating in the Treaty must intend to create a permanent law. This intention need not be expressly stated, but may be inferred from the treaty. The background, *travaux preperatoire*, preambles, and the texts of outer space treaties unequivocally indicate that the states that negotiated and concluded the treaties intended to create permanent legal obligations as regards their activities in outer space. It is, therefore, difficult to endorse the view that on the outbreak of hostilities, application of the Outer Space Treaty will be suspended and states may place nuclear or other mass-destruction weapons in outer space and militarise celestial bodies as well, because Article IV of the Treaty is concerned with disarmament and demilitarisation.[36] Although the effect of Article IV is to control specific arms in outer space, the Outer Space Treaty as a whole was adopted to create a permanent legal regime.

Concluding remarks

In addition to the treaties specifically adopted to address outer space activities, certain general international law norms, especially those concerning the use of force, self-defence, and the conduct of hostilities, are relevant and applicable to outer space military activities. These norms, along with specific treaties adopted to regulate space activities, constitute the legal regime governing the militarisation of outer space. After all, one of the most significant factors motivating states to venture into outer space was to gain military superiority and serve their strategic interests. Like any other spatial zone, outer space is bound to be a place where military confrontation between states may occur. The increasing reliance on satellites in outer space to manage day-to-day terrestrial activities may tempt states to use military force against their adversaries' outer space assets in situations of tension. Such use of military force will undoubtedly pose a significant threat to international peace and security everywhere. Against this background, the next chapter examines current and projected military activities in outer space.

References

Arms Control Association, 'Russia Withdraws Ratification of Nuclear Test Ban Treaty', (2 November 2023). https://www.armscontrol.org/blog/2023-11/nuclear-disarmament-monitor Accessed 25 November 2025.

Bernhardt, R., ed., *Max Planck Encyclopaedias of Public International Law*, vol. 7. Oxford: Oxford University Press, 1985.

35 Ibid., 723.

36 A. J. Butler, 'Peaceful Use and Self-Defense in Outer Space', *Proceedings of the Twenty-Fifth Colloquium on the Law of Outer Space*, (1982), 80.

Bowett D. W., *Self-Defence in International Law*. New York: Praeger, 1958.

Brownlie I., *International Law and Use of Force by States*. Oxford: Oxford University Press, 1968.

Brownlie I., 'The Maintenance of Peace and Security in Outer Space', *British Yearbook of International Law*, 40 (1964), 1–31.

Butler A. J., 'Peaceful Use and Self-Defense in Outer Space', *Proceedings of the Twenty-Fifth Colloquium on the Law of Outer Space*, (1982), 80.

Cheng B., 'The Extraterrestrial Application of International Law', *Current Legal Problems*, 18 (1965), 132–52.

Gal G., *Space Law*. Leiden: A.W. Sijthoff, 1969.

Harris D. J., *Cases and Materials on International Law*. London: Sweet & Maxwell, 1983.

ICRC, 'Outer Space Weapons and International Humanitarian Law'. https://www.icrc.org/en/law-and-policy/weapons-outer-space Accessed 25 November 2025.

Lachs M., *The Law of Outer Space: An Experience in Contemporary Law Making*. Leiden: A.W. Sijthof, 1972.

Loon F., 'Codifying *Jus in Bello Spatialis*: The Space Law of Tomorrow', *Strategic Studies Quarterly*, 15 (2021), 10–27.

McNair A. D., *The Law of Treaties*. Oxford: Oxford University Press, 1961.

Melzer N., *International Humanitarian Law: A Comprehensive Introduction*. Geneva: ICRC, 2016.

Military and Paramilitary Activities in and against Nicaragua Case (Nicaragua v. United States) (Merits) *I.C.J. Reports*, 1986. http://www.icj-cij.org/docket/files/70/6503.pdf Accessed 25 November 2025.

Oil Platforms Case (Iran v. United States), 2003. http://www.icj-cij.org/docket/files/90/9715.pdf Accessed 25 November 2025.

Prosecutor v. Dusko Tadic aka "Dule" (Decision on the Defence Motion for Interlocutory Appeal on Jurisdiction), IT-94–1. International Criminal Tribunal for the Former Yugoslavia (ICTY), 2 October 1995. https://www.refworld.org/jurisprudence/caselaw/icty/1995/en/61438 Accessed 25 November 2025.

Rome Statute of the International Criminal Court. UN *Treaty Collection*, vol. 2187-I-38544.

UN GA Res. 3314 (XXIX), 14 December 1974.

UN *Treaty Collection*, vol. 480-I-6964.

UNGA Res. 1721 (XVI).

UNGA Res. 1962 (XVIII).

3 Military activities in outer space

Today, after nearly seven decades of space exploration, outer space is extensively used for a variety of military activities. They have implications for safety and security in outer space, on celestial bodies, in airspace, and on Earth's surface. Conversely, military activities conducted in airspace and on Earth's surface may pose safety and security risks to human operations in outer space and on celestial bodies. Some of these activities are already underway, some are at various stages of development, while others are futuristic, though not entirely unrealistic. Many terrestrial and extraterrestrial military activities are inseparably linked. This chapter aims to outline and explain the basic features of all these activities.

Military satellites

Satellites in outer space perform a variety of military functions. Since the early days of space exploration, these applications of outer space have become quite common. These are outlined in the following.

Reconnaissance satellites

As concepts of state sovereignty and state jurisdiction were crystallised in international relations and law, espionage, which involves entering another state's territorial domain, was recognised as a serious crime in national legal systems, with the most common punishment being execution. Collection of military intelligence without entering a state's territorial domain, that is, from international airspace, the high seas, or the territory of the collecting state, may be termed 'extraterritorial espionage'. To facilitate this, sophisticated technology has been developed over time. With the advent of man in outer space, substantial emphasis was placed on the development and articulation of satellite reconnaissance.

Many countries have developed and deployed satellites equipped with powerful cameras that can capture detailed images from space. They detect,

DOI: 10.4324/9781003754428-4

locate, and identify military targets.[1] These satellites might also be equipped with video cameras, multispectral scanners, and microwave radars.[2] As early as the 1970s, the United States' and the Soviet Union's photo-reconnaissance satellites were able to distinguish objects smaller than 30 cm from an altitude of 185 km or more.[3] With advances in remote sensing technology, electronic equipment capable of detecting data from outer space has been developed and deployed on orbiting satellites to gather information on a range of military activities of potential adversaries, such as missile testing, radar stations, armament depots, troop movements and concentrations, nuclear explosions, and more. They are also used for threat assessment. Thus, satellite reconnaissance has become one of the most common military activities in outer space today.

Military communication satellites

Satellites are highly valuable for telecommunication. Many states have satellites in outer space, including those in low Earth orbit and geostationary orbit, which are widely used for military communication. For example, the United States has the Military Strategic and Tactical Relay (Milstar) Satellite System, which includes a constellation of five geostationary satellites.[4] The United Kingdom operates a network of four satellites that comprise its Skynet military satellite system.[5] This system is managed by Astrium Services, a private provider of civil and military space services with almost worldwide coverage.[6] Generally, military communication satellites operate in ultra-high frequency, super-high frequency, or extremely high frequency bands. Many countries lack dedicated satellites for military communication. They utilise their communication satellites for both civilian and military purposes.

Military navigation satellites

Navigation satellites transmit coded signals that enable armed forces to determine their positions with high precision.[7] These satellites can also detect

1 Bhupendra Jasani, 'Outer Space Militarisation Outpaces Legal Controls', in Nandasiri Jasentuliyana, ed., *Maintaining Outer Space for Peaceful Uses* (New York: United Nations University, 1984), 222.

2 Ibid.

3 B. G. Blair, 'Reconnaissance Satellites', in Bhupendra Jasani, ed., *Outer Space: A New Dimension of Arms Race* (London: Routledge, 1982), 130.

4 *Global Security*, https://www.globalsecurity.org/military/library/budget/fy2000/dot-e/airforce/00milstar.html#google_vignette Accessed 23 November 2025.

5 *Skynet Coverage*, https://web.archive.org/web/20140516082649/http://www.satcom-airbusds.com/products-solutions/government-satcom/products-systems/bandwidth/skynet-5-x-band/#satellite-coverage-skynet-5-x-band Accessed 23 November 2025.

6 Ibid.

7 Jasani, 'Outer Space Militarisation', 225.

nuclear explosions and provide data for damage assessment during and after a nuclear attack.[8] The functions of these satellites are coordinated and managed by Global Navigation Satellite Systems (GNSS), which consist of constellations of Earth-orbiting satellites. Although navigation satellites serve various civilian purposes, such as telecommunications, land surveying, law enforcement, emergency response, precision agriculture, mining, finance, and scientific research, they are also widely utilised for military purposes. Today, the Global Positioning System (GPS), which depends on navigation satellites, has become an essential military resource.[9] It is effective in synchronising operations, providing navigation information, identifying targets, and locating personnel.[10]

Early warning satellites

Military early warning satellites detect missile launches, space launches, and nuclear detonations. The United States Space Force's early warning satellite system, known as 'Defense Support Program', utilises infrared sensors to detect heat from missile and booster plumes against Earth's background.[11] They deliver precise, trustworthy data on missile threats to the United States and its allies.[12] Situated in geostationary orbit, they offer complete hemispheric coverage.[13] The Russian equivalent of early warning satellites is called the 'EKS Kupol' system.[14] Furthermore, China, France, and India are believed to have space and terrestrial assets for early warning.[15]

Dual-purpose data-collecting satellites

Several satellites that collect data from outer space for civilian purposes may also provide data for military use. Satellites gathering meteorological data can measure atmospheric properties that may enhance the accuracy of missile guidance.[16] For instance, information on water vapour density and wind velocity along a missile's

8 Ibid.

9 Smithsonian: National Air and Space Museum, https://timeandnavigation.si.edu/satellite-navigation/who-uses-satellite-navigation/military-applications Accessed 23 November 2025.

10 Ibid.

11 United States Space Force, https://www.spaceforce.mil/About-Us/Fact-Sheets/Fact-Sheet-Display/Article/2197774/defense-support-program-satellites/ Accessed 23 November 2025.

12 Ibid.

13 Ibid.

14 *The Space Review*, https://www.thespacereview.com/article/4121/1 Accessed 23 November 2025.

15 Philip S. Clark, 'China's Shiyan Weixing Satellite Programme', *Space Chronicle*, 71 (2018), 22–30; *Optronique & Defence, Pea Spirale*, http://optronique.net/defense/pea/spirale Accessed 23 November 2025, and CNBC-TV18, 'ISRO Chief Opens Up about Their Big Role in India's Defence System', (12 May 2025). https://www.cnbctv18.com/india/isro-chief-opens-up-about-their-big-role-in-india-defence-system-19603085.htm Accessed 23 November 2025.

16 George M. Siouris, *Missile Guidance and Control Systems* (New York: Springer, 2004), 99–100.

potential flight path would be essential to improving attack accuracy.[17] Geodetic satellites can also be helpful for military applications. Geodesy is an operation that gathers geophysical data used to determine the size and shape of the Earth, its gravitational field, and to provide detailed maps and locations on the globe of cities, towns, and villages, as well as the positions of military targets.[18] Data collected by such satellites are helpful for both civilian and military purposes.

Space weapons

By space weapons, we mean weapons or objects that are capable of (a) causing damage, destruction or in any other manner rendering useless objects located in outer space or on celestial bodies from outer space or celestial bodies; (b) causing damage, destruction, or in any other manner rendering useless objects located in airspace, the seas, or terrestrial Earth from outer space or celestial bodies; and (c) causing damage, destruction, or in any other manner rendering useless objects located in outer space or on celestial bodies from the airspace, the seas, or the terrestrial Earth. Therefore, they comprise space-to-space, space-to-Earth, and Earth-to-space weapons. According to some countries, Earth-to-space weapons are not classified as 'space weapons'.[19] However, for this work, any device that can potentially cause damage or destruction in outer space or on celestial bodies is regarded as a space weapon, regardless of its location. In the previous definition, destruction means the damaging of both non-living and living objects, including causing injury or death to humans. They do not include ballistic missiles that may pass through outer space without completing a full orbit. Space weapons can be either defensive or offensive. They can be either kinetic or non-kinetic. They are meant to inflict physical damage through impact from a substance or energy, or operational damage by rendering a space object useless without causing physical harm.

On 23 March 1983, President Ronald Reagan delivered a famous speech and announced the initiation of a significant space defence programme.[20] He emphasised the importance of establishing a defensive system against hostile missile attacks with the following words:

> What if free people could live secure in the knowledge that their security did not rest upon the threat of instant US retaliation to deter a Soviet

17 Ani Stefanova, 'The Role of Geodesy in Military Operations: Historical Developments and Modern Use', *Security and Defence*, 1 (2025), 216. https://journals.indexcopernicus.com/api/file/viewByFileId/2412110#:~:text=Military%20engineers%20used%20geodetic%20data,of%20military%20strategy%20and%20tactics Accessed 28 November 2025.

18 Ibid.

19 Todd Harrison, 'Defining Space Warfare and Space Weapons', *International Perspectives on Space Weapons: A Report* (Washington, DC: Centre for Strategic and International Studies, 2020), 4.

20 *The New York Times* (24 March 1983), 20.

> attack; that we could intercept and destroy strategic ballistic missiles before they reached our own soil or that of our allies?

He further addressed the scientific community:

> I call upon the scientific community in our country, those who gave us nuclear weapons to turn their great talents now to the cause of mankind and world peace; to give us the means of rendering these nuclear weapons impotent and obsolete.[21]

The SDI was launched at a time when the United States and the Soviet Union were staunch adversaries. The political developments of the 1990s – particularly the collapse of the Soviet Union – led to significant changes in the United States' defence strategy. It is believed that the Soviet Union launched its own version of the Strategic Defence Initiative, called the 'Polyus-Skif Orbital Weapons Platform' programme, initiated in the 1980s.[22] However, it is believed that the Soviet Union lacked the capacity to compete with the United States in military superiority and that its leaders bluffed about their technological capabilities.[23]

In light of the dissolution of the Soviet Union and subsequent budgetary constraints, President George H.W. Bush authorised a scaled-back Global Protection Against Limited Strikes (GPALS) programme in 1991.[24] This programme involved the so-called 'brilliant pebbles' – small, lightweight spacecraft that could intercept advanced missiles by colliding with them at high speed during the boost phase.[25] It was expected that a worldwide network of small satellites would intercept hostile missiles on command without any external assistance.[26] This was justified considering the increase in nuclear and other weapons of mass destruction and their means of delivery.[27] Apart from the Russian Federation, the United States was especially concerned about countries like China, the Democratic People's Republic of North Korea (DPRK), and Iran acquiring technology to develop nuclear or other weapons

21 Ibid.

22 *New Space Economy*, 'The Secret Soviet Quest for Space-based Weapons', (27 May 2024). https://newspaceeconomy.ca/2024/05/27/the-secret-soviet-quest-for-space-based-weapons/ Accessed 23 November 2025.

23 Jon Agor, *Science Policy Under Thatcher* (London: Palgrave Macmillan, 2019), 209.

24 Mallory Stewart, 'The Strategic Defence Initiative in Retrospect: The Past, Present and Future of Missile Defense', *US Department of State*, (April 2023). https://www.state.gov/the-strategic-defense-initiative-in-retrospect-the-past-present-and-future-of-missile-defense/ Accessed 23 November 2025.

25 Lawrence Livermore National Laboratory, 'Adapting to a Changing Weapons Program', *Science & Technology Review*, (January 2001). https://www.llnl.gov/archives/1980s/brilliant-pebbles Accessed 23 November 2025.

26 Ibid.

27 Stewart, 'The Strategic Defence Initiative'.

of mass destruction and improve their delivery systems with greater range and accuracy. In addition, following the rising threat of terrorist attacks against the United States and its allies, the fear of nuclear weapons and missiles falling into the hands of terrorist organisations was palpable.

The next significant development in the evolution of the United States' missile defence policy was the launch of a ballistic missile defence programme in 1999, called '3-Plus-3' and later a '3-Plus-5' programme, by President Bill Clinton, with the adoption of the National Missile Defence Act.[28] As nuclear and other weapons of mass destruction, along with their delivery systems, continued to proliferate, the United States, under President George W. Bush, withdrew from the Anti-Ballistic Missile Treaty in 2002 and began deploying the 'Ground-based Midcourse Defense System' at Fort Greely, Alaska, and Vandenberg, California, in 2004.[29] As the rapprochement between many former Soviet allies and the West became a reality, the United States decided to deploy components of its missile defence in Poland and the Czech Republic, signing legally binding agreements to that end.[30] These 'Third Site' agreements were replaced in 2009 by the Obama administration with the adoption of the 'European Phased Adaptive Approach' (EPAA) policy that favoured NATO-based deployments in Romania and Poland.[31] Today, the U.S. missile defence policy's primary focus is on developing and deploying missile defence system components within the territories of its allies and partners.[32]

Almost immediately after the start of his second term, President Trump proposed a missile defence shield programme called 'Golden Dome for America'.[33] It is expected to be a comprehensive anti-missile and air defence system designed to protect the United States against future threats from ballistic, hypersonic, and advanced cruise missiles, as well as other sophisticated aerial attacks from hostile states.[34] It is designed as a layered system comprising interceptors and various space and land-based support systems for intelligence and warning, attack assessment, battle management, command, control, and communications, as well as trans-attack and/or post-attack response.[35] In April 2025, the Pentagon reported receiving interest from around

28 Ibid.
29 Ibid.
30 Ibid.
31 Ibid.
32 Ibid.
33 Stephen J. Cimbala and Lawrence J. Korb, 'Trump's Iron Dome for America Is Ambitious: It Also Has Some Serious Technology and Policy Flaws', *Bulletin of the Atomic Scientists*, 81 (28 February 2025). https://thebulletin.org/2025/02/trumps-iron-dome-for-america-is-ambitious-it-also-has-some-serious-technology-and-policy-flaws/ Accessed 23 November 2025.
34 Ibid.
35 Ibid.

180 companies eager to develop the so-called 'Golden Dome', including Elon Musk's SpaceX.[36] In May 2025, it was reported that President Trump had selected a design for the $175 billion Golden Dome missile defence shield and had inaugurated the programme.[37]

Like the United States, the Russian space weapons programme has experienced many ups and downs. It was initiated during the Soviet era. Immediately after the dissolution of the Soviet Union, Russia faced the challenge of maintaining the programme it inherited and preventing the deterioration of its space infrastructure.[38] During the 2000s, although Russia's interest in space grew, its focus shifted from military to commercial launches.[39] However, another report suggests that during the same decade, Russia continued active military space programmes in early warning, optical reconnaissance, communication, navigation, and signal intelligence.[40] Although there is limited reporting on the Russian military space programme, it seems that Russia was closely observing developments in the United States and keeping up with them. Despite some setbacks, the size of the Russian space programme, its infrastructure, and the expertise gained since the Soviet era establish Russia as a key player in the process of weaponising outer space.[41] If media reports from May 2024 about Russia's launch of a satellite with anti-satellite capabilities in low Earth orbit are correct, they confirm Russia's ongoing interest in the space weapons programme.[42]

Apart from the veteran space powers, the United States and Russia, other countries also harbour ambitions to develop anti-satellite weapon technology. It is believed that the United States' Aegis anti-satellite technology is being jointly developed with Japan and will be operated by both of them.[43] Once fully developed, this technology is likely to be transferred to the United States' European allies and to South Korea.[44] Additionally,

36 Mike Stone and Marisa Taylor, 'Musk's SpaceX Is Forerunner to Build Trump's Golden Dome Missile Shield', *Reuters*, (17 April 2025). https://www.reuters.com/business/aerospace-defense/musks-spacex-is-frontrunner-build-trumps-golden-dome-missile-shield-2025-04-17/ Accessed 23 November 2025.

37 Mike Stone and Jeff Mason, 'Trump Selects $175 Billion Golden Dome Defense Shield Design, Appoints Leader', *Reuters*, (21 May 2025). https://www.reuters.com/world/us/trump-make-golden-dome-announcement-tuesday-us-official-says-2025-05-20/ Accessed 23 November 2025.

38 Pavel Podvig and Hui Zhang, *Russian and Chinese Responses to US Military Plans in Space* (Cambridge, MA: American Academy of Arts and Sciences, 2008), 5.

39 Laura Grego, 'A History of Anti-Satellite Programs', *Union of Concerned Scientists*, Cambridge MA, (January 2012). https://www.ucs.org/sites/default/files/2019-09/a-history-of-ASAT-programs_lo-res.pdf Accessed 25 November 2025.

40 Podvig and Zhang, *Russian and Chinese Responses*, 5.

41 Ibid., 26.

42 Jaroslav Lukiv, 'US Says Russia Likely Launched Anti-Satellite Weapon', *BBC News*, (22 May 2024). https://www.bbc.com/news/articles/cq55ww5j7e2o Accessed 23 November 2025.

43 Grego, 'A History of Anti-Satellite Programs', 12.

44 Ibid.

China demonstrated anti-satellite capabilities in 2007, and India showcased them in 2019.[45] Against this backdrop, the following outlines various space weapons technologies being developed by leading space-faring states and other entities.

Kinetic energy weapons

A kinetic energy weapon causes a forceful impact on a target by a solid or explosive substance that is directed at the target and released from a launching device. Such weapons may be direct-ascent weapons, that is, weapons located on Earth but designed to destroy targets in outer space. A direct-ascent anti-satellite (ASAT) weapon consists of an interceptor launched on a missile and released against the target satellite. It might release a cloud of pellets to boost the likelihood of colliding with the target satellite before interception. They are intended to be more effective against low Earth orbit (LEO) satellites due to their limited range.[46]

Another type of kinetic energy ASAT weapon is co-orbital, meaning those that are based aboard a space platform or a satellite launched into the same orbit as the target satellite. They are supposed to approach the target satellite and deploy explosives aimed at it. They can also use unguided clouds of pellets or homing interceptors, which are launched shortly before the attack.[47] It is believed that such ASAT weapons have the advantage of being camouflaged, providing the target with limited warning before an attack.[48]

The Soviet Union was engaged in developing anti-satellite capabilities, likely involving kinetic energy, from the early days of space exploration as a response to the United States' anti-satellite weapons programme of the 1960s and 1970s.[49] In response to the United States announcement of the SDI, the Soviet Union restarted research on space-based ASAT and anti-ballistic missile defence systems.[50] After inheriting the Soviet space programme, Russia chose

45 See generally, Dimitrios Stroikos, 'Still Lost in Space? Understanding China and India's Anti-Satellite Tests Through an Eclectic Approach', *International Journal of Space Politics and Policy*, 21 (2023), 181–205. https://www.tandfonline.com/doi/full/10.1080/14777622.2023.2277253 Accessed 23 November 2025.

46 Nivedita Raju, 'A Proposal for a Ban on Destructive Anti-Satellite Testing: A Role for the European Union?', *Non-Proliferation and Disarmament Papers*, 74 (2021), 1–15. https://www.sipri.org/publications/2021/eu-non-proliferation-and-disarmament-papers/proposal-ban- destructive-anti-satellite-testing-role-european-union Accessed 23 November 2025.

47 Ibid.

48 Ibid.

49 Khyati Singh, 'Russia's Resurgence in Space: Anti-Satellite Capabilities and Tests', *Centre for Air Power Studies*, (26 February 2024). https://capsindia.org/russias-resurgence-in-space-anti-satellite-capabilities-tests/ Accessed 23 November 2025.

50 Grego, 'A History of Anti-Satellite Programs', 5.

to diversify its anti-satellite weapons programme, although it still maintains an interest in kinetic energy weapons for space applications.[51] It is believed that Russia carried out several ASAT weapons tests using direct-ascent technology in the 2010s.[52] These tests are ongoing. In November 2021, Russia reportedly tested a direct-ascent anti-satellite kinetic energy missile.[53] It is claimed that this highly destructive weapons test forced astronauts aboard the International Space Station to take shelter and generated a long-lasting field of space debris.[54]

Alongside anti-satellite kinetic energy weapons programmes, ballistic missile defence test programmes began in the 1980s. In February 1987, it was announced that the Strategic Defence Initiative Organisation was close to developing a cost-effective space-based kinetic-kill vehicle capable of destroying intercontinental ballistic missiles during various phases.[55] Although testing of kinetic energy weapons slowed during the 1990s, it was revived in the 2000s. The United States conducted 76 ballistic missile defence tests using kinetic energy devices between 2001 and 2013.[56]

The United States conducted its first sea-based anti-satellite kinetic energy weapon test in 2008, destroying one of its defunct satellites.[57] China had already successfully tested an ASAT kinetic energy device in 2007 and had begun exploring ballistic missile defence capabilities around that time.[58] The 2007 Chinese test generated over 2,500 pieces of trackable debris, increasing the number of man-made objects in space by 20 per cent and thereby raising the likelihood of collisions by 37 per cent.[59] It is also believed that this test has produced about 150000 non-trackable pieces of debris.[60] It is argued that if this debris were to harm another state's space assets, China could be entirely responsible for all damage caused under the Liability Convention.[61]

51 Singh, 'Russia's Resurgence'.

52 Raju, 'A Proposal for a Ban', 4.

53 Erin Pobjie, 'The Threat from Outer Space: Russia Tests Kinetic DA-ASAT Weapon', *Just Security*, (23 November 2021). https://www.justsecurity.org/79320/the-threat-from-outer-space-russia-tests-kinetic-da-asat-weapon/ Accessed 23 November 2025.

54 Ibid.

55 U.S. Department of Defense, *Report to the Congress on Strategic Defense Initiative*, April 1987, VI-D-1.

56 Michael Krepon and Sonya Shoenberger, *Anti-Satellite Weapons, Deterrence and Sino-American Space Relations: A Report* (Washington, DC: Stimson Center, 2013), 131.

57 Ibid.

58 Ibid.

59 Jeffrey L. Caton, 'Impacts of Anti-Access/Area Denial Measures on Space Systems: Issues and Implications for Army and Joint Forces', (Carlisle: U.S. Army War College Press, 2018), 1. http://www.jstor.com/stable/resrep20087 Accessed 23 November 2025. Also see, Raju, 'A Proposal for a Ban', 4.

60 Raju, 'A Proposal for a Ban', 4.

61 Danylo Stonis, 'Ambiguities in Space Law as Path Towards Weaponisation of Space: The Case of the Outer Space Treaty', *Copernicus Political and Legal Studies*, 1 (2022), 82.

In March 2019, India successfully conducted a test of a kinetic anti-satellite weapon called 'Shakti'.[62] During this test, India employed the Defence Research and Development Organisation's ballistic missile defence interceptor as a kinetic anti-satellite missile.[63] This test generated hundreds of pieces of debris, despite Indian authorities' claims that it was conducted at a low Earth orbit of 300 km, intended to produce less debris and prevent harm to other satellites above this orbit. Nevertheless, the weapon could destroy a satellite at an altitude of 1000 km.[64]

Electromagnetic railgun

An electromagnetic railgun is a specialised form of kinetic energy weapon. A railgun bullet is expected to travel at a velocity several times higher than that of a cruise missile.[65] Such guns were being developed not only for use in outer space but also for terrestrial applications, including the seas. Their ultra-high speed is believed to be due to electromagnetic thrust. They were designed for use in long-range strikes, strategic air defence, and ballistic missile defence.[66] In February 2024, reports suggested that China had successfully tested an electromagnetic railgun.[67] In October 2022, it was reported that India was working on an electromagnetic railgun.[68] Although there is no evidence to suggest that the Soviet Union had begun developing electromagnetic railguns, Russia is reported to have successfully developed the technology to produce them.[69]

Killer satellites

The Soviet Union began its ASAT weapons programme in the 1960s. During that period, its focus was on Kamikaze-style 'killer' or 'hunter-killer' satellites

62 Singh, 'Russia's Resurgence in Space'.

63 Ibid.

64 Raju, 'A Proposal for a Ban', 5

65 Weiwei Mao, Teng Pang, Zhirong Guo, Hongbao Bai, Zhixiong Huang, and Xiaoyu Jin, 'Analysis of the Research Progress of Electromagnetic Railgun Based on CiteSpace', *IEEE Access*, 20 (2017), 1. https://www.researchgate.net/publication/377071631_Analysis_of_the_Research_Progress_of_Electromagnetic_Railgun_Based_on_CiteSpace Accessed 23 November 2025.

66 Ibid.

67 Parth Satam, 'Scrapped by US Navy after $500M Investment, China "Succeeds" in Electromagnetic Railgun-Fired "Smart Shell" – Reports', *The EurAsian Times*, (9 February 2024). https://www.eurasiantimes.com/railgun-fired-smart-dream-shell-but-us-spent-500/ Accessed 23 November 2025.

68 Indian Defence Research and Development Organization's bulletin *Technology Focus's* vol. 30, No. 5 of October 2022 exclusively deals with India's electromagnetic railgun project. https://www.drdo.gov.in/drdo/sites/default/files/technology-focus-documrnt/TF_October2022.pdf Accessed 23 November 2025.

69 *Global Defence News*, 'Russia Continues R&D work on Electromagnetic Railgun', (23 January 2018). https://www.armyrecognition.com/news/navy-news/2018/russia-continues-r-d-work-on-electromagnetic-railgun#google_vignette Accessed 23 November 2025.

designed to approach their target satellite and explode nearby, thereby damaging or destroying it.[70] The damage mechanism involved chemical non-nuclear explosives.[71] During the post-Soviet era, Russia continued the programme that simultaneously focused on ASAT and anti-missile capabilities.[72] However, it was kept secret until 2009, when Russia disclosed it to the international community as a response to the Chinese and United States ASAT weapons tests of 2007 and 2008, respectively.[73] It is also suggested that small satellites, known as 'micro-satellites', could act as 'space mines'. There are reports of tests conducted by Russia in 2020 in which Russian satellites ejected subsatellites or other objects into orbit.[74] Most probably, they belong to the category of hunter-killer satellites. The United States Global Protection Against Limited Strikes (GPALS) – 'Brilliant Pebbles' – programme probably qualifies as a killer satellite programme, as it involves a global network of small satellites for its destructive system.

Directed energy weapons

Directed energy weapons (DEWs) are devices that emit a concentrated beam of electromagnetic energy that can damage objects and harm individuals. These weapons include high-energy lasers and particle beams that emit energy to cause damage. The beams are designed to transmit energy from the source to the target.[75]

A beam of light amplification by stimulated emission of radiation (Laser) is produced by stimulating atoms or molecules.[76] The United States declassified some of its reports regarding space lasers in March 1982.[77] In 1987, it was reported that the Soviet Union had been developing very powerful laser weapons since 1978, capable of damaging satellites at altitudes of up to

70 Marcia Smith, 'Satellite and Missile ASAT Systems and Potential Verification Problems Associated with the Existing Soviet Systems', in Bhupendra Jasani, ed., *Space Weapons: The Arms Control Dilemma* (Stockholm: SIPRI, 1984), 84.

71 Ibid.

72 *TASS*, 'Russian Anti-Satellite System'. https://www.russianspaceweb.com/naryad.html Accessed 23 November 2025.

73 Ibid.

74 Raju, 'A Proposal for a Ban', 4.

75 U.S. Government Accountability Office, 'Science and Tech Spotlight: Directed Energy Weapons: Fact Sheet', (25 May 2023). https://www.gao.gov/assets/gao-23-106717.pdf Accessed 23 November 2025.

76 *Britannica*, https://www.britannica.com/technology/laser Accessed 23 November 2025.

77 U.S. General Accounting Office, 'Statement by Donald E. Day, Senior Associate Director, Mission Analysis and Systems Acquisition Division, before the Subcommittee on Strategic and Theatre Nuclear Forces, Committee of Armed Services, United States Senate on Space-based Lasers', (16 March 1982). https://www.gao.gov/assets/117803.pdf Accessed 23 November 2025.

40,000 km.[78] Russia has inherited the Soviet Union's quite advanced laser programme, begun in the 1970s, and has continued it diligently. It is believed that China's efforts to develop laser weapons began as early as the 1960s, with most of the work overseen by the Chinese Academy of Sciences and the Commission of Science, Technology, and Industry for National Defence.[79]

To produce a laser beam, various media can be employed, such as solid, gas, liquid, dye, gas-dynamic, or chemical.[80] A nuclear detonation can also produce them. It is expected that when high energy is delivered or discharged onto the target, it will be damaged, destroyed, or exploded.[81] It was reported in 1986 that an X-ray laser weapon, powered by a nuclear explosion, played a key role in the United States Strategic Defence Initiative programme.[82] In March 2025, the U.S. announced plans to strengthen national security satellites by funding a space laser programme in response to China and Russia's push to develop more anti-satellite weapons.[83]

Particle beam weapons have many similarities to laser weapons. To generate a particle beam, either electrically charged or neutral particles are required.[84] The destruction of a target using a charged particle beam can be achieved through various impact effects, such as hole boring, rupture from internal pressure, heat generation, X-rays, and electric currents that damage sensitive electronics, the initiation of detonation of high explosives, and similar effects.[85]

High-powered microwave amplification by stimulated emission of radiation (Maser) weapons are similar to laser weapons. They can be used to disrupt a satellite's electronics, corrupt data stored in memory, cause processors to restart, and, at higher power levels, inflict permanent damage on electrical circuits and processors.[86]

The military potential of directed energy weapons is very high. Their lethality depends on the amount of energy transmitted from the source to the

78 *The New York Times*, 'General Describes Soviet Laser Threat', (24 October 1987), Section 1, 62.

79 Eric Heginbotham, Michael Nixon, Forrest E. Morgan, Jacob L. Heim, Jeff Hagen, Sheng Li, Jeffrey Engstrom, Martin C. Libicki, Paul DeLuca, David A. Shlapak, David R. Frelinger, Burgess Laird, Kyle Brady, and Lyle J. Morris, *The U.S.-China Military Scorecard* (Washington, DC: RAND Corporation, 2015), 246.

80 A. M. Din, 'The Prospects of Beam Weapons', in Bhupendra Jasani, ed., *Outer Space: A New Dimension of Arms Race* (London: Routledge, 1982), 231.

81 C. N. Ghosh, 'Directed Energy Weapons', *Strategic Analysis*, XXVI (February 2001). https://ciaotest.cc.columbia.edu/olj/sa/sa_feb01ghc01.html Accessed 30 November 2025.

82 Editorial, 'X-Ray Lasers and Secrecy', *Bulletin of the Atomic Scientists*, 42 (1986), 2.

83 Matt Berman, 'The "Space Laser" Wars Have Begun – and America Wants to Be First to Develop the High-Powered Weapons', *Popular Mechanics*. https://www.popularmechanics.com/military/weapons/a64244333/space-laser-satellite/ Accessed 24 November 2025.

84 John Parmentola and Kosta Tipsis, 'Particle Beam Weapons', *Scientific American*, 240 (1979), 54.

85 Din, 'The Prospects of Beam Weapons', 233.

86 Todd Harrison, Kaitlyn Johnson, Thomas G. Roberts, Madison Bergenthon, and Alexandra Coultrup, 'Types of Counterspace Weapons', *Space Threat Assessment: A Report* (Washington, DC: Centre for Strategic and International Studies, 2019), 4.

target. They are being considered for space-to-space, space-to-Earth, and Earth-to-space applications.[87] Their intended targets are hostile satellites and ballistic missiles.[88] It is believed that, in addition to the United States, China, France, India, and Russia have made substantial advancements in directed energy weapons technology.[89]

Electromagnetic pulse weapons

Serious research into the effects of electromagnetic pulses for weapon applications began in the 1970s. A high-altitude nuclear detonation can generate gamma rays. These rays travel towards Earth's surface, and during their journey, they encounter air molecules in the upper atmosphere.[90] This produces a flash of electrons, which are accelerated and deflected by Earth's magnetic field, creating an electrically charged field over a large area and generating an electromagnetic pulse that spreads to an even broader area of the Earth's surface.[91] The pulse effect was studied in the United States during the late 1970s, and its potential as a weapon was suggested, although not developed at that time. An electromagnetic pulse can (a) devastate satellites, (b) disrupt telecommunications, and (c) destroy a satellite's communication system.[92] The effects of electromagnetic pulses include data corruption on memory chips, processor resets, and short circuits that can cause permanent damage to satellite components.[93] If a nuclear detonation generates an electromagnetic pulse, it would instantly affect satellites in its vicinity. At the same time, it would generate a high-radiation environment that would accelerate the degradation of components over time in all unshielded satellites within the affected orbital zone.[94]

In the 1970s, the Soviet Union carried out nuclear detonations at high altitude above the Sary Shagan radar system, presumably to investigate

87 Bob Preston, Dana J. Johnson, Sean J. A. Edwards, Michael Miller, and Calvin Shipbaugh, *Space Weapons Earth Wars* (Washington, DC: RAND Corporation, 2002), 24–37.

88 Ibid.

89 Clayton Swope, Kari A. Bingen, Markena Young, Madeleine Chang, Stephanie Songer, and Jeremy Tammelleo, *Space Threat Assessment 2024* (Washington, DC: Center for Strategic and International Studies, April 2024), 11–2. https://www.csis.org/analysis/space-threat-assessment-2024 Accessed 23 November 2025.

90 M. Felden, 'Recent Advances in the Use of Space for Military Purposes and on Second Generation Nuclear Weapons', in Bhupendra Jasani, ed., *Outer Space: A New Dimension of Arms Race* (London: Routledge, 1982), 258.

91 Ibid.

92 *Ocotec Oy*, 'What Does an EMP (Electromagnetic Pulse) Do?', (19 June 2024). https://ocotec.fi/en/what-does-an-emp-electromagnetic-pulse-do/ Accessed 28 November 2025.

93 Todd Harrison, Kaitlyn Johnson, and Makena Young, 'Space Defences Defined', *Defence Against the Dark Art in Space: A Report*, Centre for Strategic and International Studies (Washington, DC: Centre for Strategic and International Studies, 2021), Chapter 3.

94 Ibid.

and study the effects of electromagnetic nuclear pulses on electronic components.[95] Since those days, the United States and Russia have made significant progress in developing electromagnetic pulse technology for military use. In February 2024, the United States government confirmed that Russia is developing a new ASAT capability in the form of a nuclear weapon in space and that it is creating a nuclear-powered electronic warfare satellite.[96]

Radio-frequency weapons

Radio-frequency weapons are a type of weaponry designed to disrupt or disable an adversary's device or system by utilising the electromagnetic environment.[97] Thus, a satellite's ability to perform its functions is temporarily interrupted without causing any physical damage, as long as the target remains engaged. Attacks using radio-frequency weapons may disrupt the operation of space-based radar and the reception of signals by service users and customers on Earth, the satellite itself, or the ground station of a space system.[98] They may also involve spoofing, which tricks a receiver into believing a fake signal created by the attacker is the genuine signal it expects to receive.[99] The primary targets are the GNSS, the GPS, and communication satellites.[100] It is believed that jamming and spoofing are already occurring.[101]

Military activities of some regional agencies

Some regional agencies are especially interested in military activities in outer space. These are briefly outlined in the following.

The European Union (EU)

Since 2016, the EU has focused on space defence by adopting a Space Strategy. The initial aim was to utilise existing EU space infrastructure, such as

95 Hans Ruhle, 'Gorbachev's Star Wars', *NATO Review*, 33 (1985), 26.

96 Sandra Erwin, 'White House Confirms It Has Intelligence on Russia's Anti-Satellite Weapon, But Says No Immediate Threat', *Space News*, (15 February 2024). https://spacenews.com/white-house-confirms-it-has-intelligence-on-russians-anti-satellite-weapon-but-says-no-immediate-threat/ Accessed 23 November 2025.

97 Sam Frazier, *Radio-Frequency Weapons*, Occasional Paper: Naval Air Defence Centre Aircraft Division, US, (2000), 5.

98 Swope, et al., *Space Threat Assessment*, 4.

99 Ibid.

100 Ibid.

101 Ibid.

Galileo and Governmental Satellite Communications (GOVSATCOM), for military purposes.[102] At that time, the EU's space defence policy was evolving, and this process needed to address issues such as dependence on critical space technologies, the impact of Brexit, and the development of a common doctrine and mutual understanding of defence threats within the Union.[103] In May 2021, the EU Agency for the Space Programme was established by expanding the scope of the European Global Navigation Satellite Systems Supervisory Authority, which was founded in 2004. This was done to address the EU's growing role in space, emphasising areas such as growth, competitiveness, sustainability, and *security*.[104] Following this, in 2022, the EU recognised the need to develop a strategy for security and defence in the space domain.[105] It was adopted in March 2023.[106] The strategy, explicitly referencing Russian and Chinese space weapons programmes, emphasises the need for collaboration to protect the space domain. While it strongly advocates for sharing information and cooperating with the United Nations, NATO, the United States, and other states, it equally prioritises improving its capabilities to defend the space domain.[107]

North Atlantic Treaty Organisation (NATO)

As is widely understood, NATO is an intergovernmental collective security alliance established in April 1949, following the conclusion of the Second World War. It has 32 members – 30 in Europe and two in North America. It was founded by the North Atlantic Treaty, which is based on the core principle that its independent member states agree to defend one another against attacks from third states. Given NATO's mission, it has a considerable interest in space defence, deterrence, and security. Considering the increasing militarisation of space, especially the testing of ASAT and directed energy weapon systems by several states, as discussed earlier in this chapter, NATO members adopted a Space Policy in 2019, recognising space as a new operational

102 Solène Baudouin-Naneix and Liza Rais, 'The European Union and Space Defence', *Finabel: The European Land Force Commanders Organization*, (August 2019), 13. https://finabel.org/wp-content/uploads/2019/10/FFT_The_European_Union_and_Space_Defence_Web.pdf Accessed 23 November 2025.

103 Ibid.

104 European Union Agency for Space Programme, https://www.euspa.europa.eu/about/about-euspa Accessed 23 November 2025. Emphasis added.

105 European Commission, 'EU Space Strategy for Security and Defence for a Stronger and More Resilient Europe'. https://defence-industry-space.ec.europa.eu/eu-space/eu-space-strategy-security-and-defence_en Accessed 23 November 2025.

106 European Commission, 'European Union Space Strategy for Security and Defence', (10 March 2023), 1–17. https://ec.europa.eu/transparency/documents-register/detail?ref=JOIN(2023)9&lang=en Accessed 23 November 2025.

107 Ibid., 15–6.

domain alongside air, land, maritime, and cyberspace. In 2020, it established a Space Centre at the Allied Air Command in Ramstein, Germany.[108]

In 2021, at the Brussels Summit, NATO recognised that attacks on members' space assets, as well as attacks from space on member states' territory or terrestrial assets, pose a clear challenge to the Alliance's security and could trigger the invocation of Article 5 of the North Atlantic Treaty.[109] Incidentally, under Article 5 of the Treaty, the Parties agree that an armed attack against one or more of them shall be considered an attack against all. Accordingly, they will support the Party or Parties under attack by taking appropriate individual or collective measures, including the use of armed force, to restore and uphold the security of the North Atlantic area. The legal basis for this commitment is found in Article 51 of the UN Charter, which confirms the right of collective self-defence.

In January 2023, the NATO-accredited Space Centre of Excellence was established in Toulouse, France. The NATO centres of excellence are either multinational or national bodies established and sponsored to offer recognised expertise and experience in a particular subject area for the benefit of the Alliance.[110] Although they are not officially part of the NATO Command Structure, they maintain a functional relationship with NATO, contributing expertise through four transformational pillars: Concept development and experimentation; doctrine development and standardisation; education, training, exercises; and evaluation and analysis of lessons learned.[111] It is expected that the NATO Space Centre of Excellence in Toulouse will provide expertise on space activities to the NATO Space Centre at Ramstein.

One of the military space activities in which NATO is particularly interested is safeguarding critical space infrastructure essential for fulfilling its core mission. This includes (a) positioning, navigation, and timing for precision strikes, force tracking, or search and rescue missions; (b) early warning to ensure force protection and provide vital information on missile launches; (c) environmental monitoring to support meteorological forecasting and mission planning; (d) secure satellite communications, which are essential for missions involving consultation, command, and control; and (e) intelligence, surveillance, and reconnaissance for situational awareness, planning, and decision-making.[112] NATO is also emphasising

108 NATO, 'NATO Space Centre'. https://shape.nato.int/about/aco-capabilities2/nato-space-centre Accessed 30 November 2025.

109 NATO, 'NATO's Approach to Space', (21 March 2024). https://www.nato.int/cps/en/natohq/topics_175419.htm Accessed 23 November 2025.

110 NATO, 'NATO Centres of Excellence: Enhancing Capabilities, Interoperability, and Education', (18 July 2024). https://www.act.nato.int/article/nato-centres-of-excellence/#:~:text=Although%20not%20officially%20part%20of,%2C%20exercise%2C%20and%20evaluation%3B%20and Accessed 23 November 2025.

111 Ibid.

112 Ibid.

the exchange of information, cooperation and coordination, operational planning, training, capacity building, innovation, and crisis management.[113] Although the policy does not explicitly state it, NATO is expected to foster cooperation among member states in developing space weapon systems. If a member state's space assets are attacked, other members would likely use their space capabilities against the hostile state and its assets in space, as well as terrestrial targets, in line with their obligations under Article 5 of the North Atlantic Treaty.

Private commercial space entities and military support

Since the First Gulf War, from August 1990 to February 1991, private space capabilities have been utilised for military purposes on a commercial basis. For example, SpaceX, which operates a large constellation of small satellites in low Earth orbit, can provide military services for a fee. It is believed that Ukraine has been using SpaceX's Starlink terminals since the Russian invasion in February 2022, with the United States covering the cost.[114] SpaceX services were used for communication and targeting purposes and were not authorised for offensive uses, such as guiding combat unmanned aerial vehicles.[115] Regardless of this, SpaceX's space-based assets could be considered legitimate military targets under international humanitarian law when utilised for military purposes.[116] By applying the analogy of direct participation of civilians in hostilities under international humanitarian law, private space entities' space assets would no longer be considered legitimate military targets once they cease to provide military services.[117]

A challenge to increasing private sector involvement in space activities is that current space law is state-centric. To ensure non-governmental actors adhere to their states' international legal obligations, a robust oversight mechanism is required. Otherwise, there is a risk of a widening accountability gap as private sector space activities expand.[118]

113 Ibid.

114 Lonneke Paperkamp and Patrick Bolder, 'The Space Domain and Russia-Ukraine War', in Maaerten Rothman, et al., eds., *Reflections on Russia-Ukraine War* (Leiden: Leiden University Press, 2024), 267–8.

115 Ibid.

116 *Infra*, Chapter 4, at 81–2.

117 According to IHL norms, a civilian taking direct part in hostilities is not entitled to civilian protection as long as he/she is participating in hostilities. Civilian protection is regained on cessation of participation in hostilities. Nils Melzer, *Interpretative Guidance on the Notion of Direct Participation in Hostilities Under International Humanitarian Law* (Geneva: International Committee of the Red Cross, 2009), 83.

118 Vittoria Pierini, 'The Involvement of the Private Sector in the Militarisation of Outer Space and the Liability Problem', *Finabel: The European Land Force Commanders Organization*, (April 2025), 5–6. https://finabel.org/the-involvement-of-the-private-sector-in-the-militarisation-of-outer-space-and-the-liability-problem/ Accessed 23 November 2025.

Concluding remarks

The aforementioned survey of military activities in outer space shows that the militarisation of space is rapidly increasing. Satellite technology is being increasingly used for military purposes. Dependence on military space infrastructure is so significant that any interference, let alone an attack, on such space assets could result in devastating consequences. Even civilian satellites have become crucial for delivering a wide range of essential services. Any disruption to this space infrastructure would cripple civilian life. The vital role of civilian and military space assets has propelled the advancement of space weapons. Among all aspects of space militarisation, space weaponisation is the most alarming. The three main players in this field are the United States, Russia, and China. Regional organisations and space agencies, like the EU, ESA, and NATO, are coordinating efforts to promote space security and defence among their member states. Private space entities are also offering military services during times of armed conflict.

The rising geopolitical tensions have led the three primary space powers to believe that conflict in space is likely unavoidable and within technological reach. As shown in the survey above, new capabilities to destroy or disable space infrastructure, as well as terrestrial infrastructure from space, are now a reality. This poses a serious threat to international peace, security, and stability.

References

Agor J., *Science Policy Under Thatcher*. London: Palgrave Macmillan, 2019.

Baudouin-Naneix S. and Rais L., 'The European Union and Space Defence', *Finabel: The European Land Force Commanders Organization*, (August 2019). https://finabel.org/wp-content/uploads/2019/10/FFT_The_European_Union_and_Space_Defence_Web.pdf Accessed 23 November 2025.

Berman M., 'The "Space Laser" Wars Have Begun – and America Wants to Be First to Develop the High-Powered Weapons', *Popular Mechanics*. https://www.popularmechanics.com/military/weapons/a64244333/space-laser-satellite/ Accessed 24 November 2025.

Blair B. G., 'Reconnaissance Satellites', in Jasani B., ed., *Outer Space: A New Dimension of Arms Race*. London: Routledge, 1982, 125–34.

Britannica. https://www.britannica.com/technology/laser Accessed 23 November 2025.

Caton J. L., 'Impacts of Anti-Access/Area Denial Measures on Space Systems: Issues and Implications for Army and Joint Forces', (US Army War College Press, Carlisle, 2018). http://www.jstor.com/stable/resrep20087 Accessed 23 November 2025.

Cimbala S. J. and Korb L. J., 'Trump's Iron Dome for America Is Ambitious: It Also Has Some Serious Technology and Policy Flaws', *Bulletin of the Atomic Scientists*, (28 February 2025). https://thebulletin.org/2025/02/trumps-iron-dome-for-america-is-ambitious-it-also-has-some-serious-technology-and-policy-flaws/ Accessed 23 November 2025.

Clark P. S., 'China's Shiyan Weixing Satellite Programme', *Space Chronicle*, 71 (2018), 22–30. *Optronique & Defence, Pea Spirale*. http://optronique.net/defense/pea/spirale Accessed 23 November 2025.

CNBC-TV18, 'ISRO Chief Opens Up about Their Big Role in India's Defence System', (12 May 2025). https://www.cnbctv18.com/india/isro-chief-opens-up-about-their-big-role-in-india-defence-system-19603085.htm Accessed 23 November 2025.

'Defence Research and Development Organization', *Technology Focus*, 30 (2022). https://www.drdo.gov.in/drdo/sites/default/files/technology-focus-documrnt/TF_October2022.pdf Accessed 23 November 2025.

Din A. M., 'The Prospects of Beam Weapons', in Jasani B., ed., *Outer Space: A New Dimension of Arms Race*. London: Routledge, 1982, 229–40.

Editorial, 'X-Ray Lasers and Secrecy', *Bulletin of the Atomic Scientists*, 42 (1986), 2.

Erwin S., 'White House Confirms It Has Intelligence on Russia's Anti-Satellite Weapon, But Says No Immediate Threat', *Space News*, (15 February 2024). https://spacenews.com/white-house-confirms-it-has-intelligence-on-russians-anti-satellite-weapon-but-says-no-immediate-threat/ Accessed 23 November 2025.

European Commission, 'EU Space Strategy for Security and Defence for a Stronger and More Resilient Europe'. https://defence-industry-space.ec.europa.eu/eu-space/eu-space-strategy-security-and-defence_en Accessed 23 November 2025.

European Commission, 'European Union Space Strategy for Security and Defence', (10 March 2023). https://ec.europa.eu/transparency/documents-register/detail?ref=JOIN(2023)9&lang=en Accessed 23 November 2025.

European Union Agency for Space Programme, https://www.euspa.europa.eu/about/about-euspa Accessed 23 November 2025.

Felden M., 'Recent Advances in the Use of Space for Military Purposes and on Second Generation Nuclear Weapons', in Jasani B., ed., *Outer Space: A New Dimension of Arms Race*. London: Routledge, 1982, 257–64.

Frazier S., *Radio-Frequency Weapons*, Occasional Paper: The United States Naval Air Defence Centre Aircraft Division, Patuxent River, MD (2000).

Ghosh C. N., 'Directed Energy Weapons', *Strategic Analysis*, XXVI (February 2001). https://ciaotest.cc.columbia.edu/olj/sa/sa_feb01ghc01.html Accessed 30 November 2025.

Global Defence News, 'Russia Continues R&D work on Electromagnetic Railgun', (23 January 2018). https://www.armyrecognition.com/news/navy-news/2018/russia-continues-r-d-work-on-electromagnetic-railgun#google_vignette Accessed 23 November 2025.

Global Security, https://www.globalsecurity.org/military/library/budget/fy2000/dot-e/airforce/00milstar.html#google_vignette Accessed 23 November 2025.

Grego L., 'A History of Anti-Satellite Programs', *Union of Concerned Scientists*, Cambridge, MA, (January 2012). https://www.ucs.org/sites/default/files/2019-09/a-history-of-ASAT-programs_lo-res.pdf Accessed 25 November 2025.

Harrison T., 'Defining Space Warfare and Space Weapons', *International Perspectives on Space Weapons: A Report*. Washington, DC: Centre for Strategic and International Studies, 2020.

Harrison T., Johnson K., Roberts T. G., et al., 'Types of Counterspace Weapons', *Space Threat Assessment: A Report*. Washington, DC: Centre for Strategic and International Studies, 2019.

Harrison T., Johnson K. and Young M., 'Space Defences Defined', *Defence Against the Dark Art in Space: A Report*. Washington, DC: Centre for Strategic and International Studies, 2021.

Heginbotham E., Nixon M., Morgan F. E., et al., *The U.S.-China Military Scorecard*. Washington, DC: RAND Corporation, 2015.

Jasani B., 'Outer Space Militarisation Outpaces Legal Controls', in Jasentuliyana N., ed., *Maintaining Outer Space for Peaceful Uses*. New York: United Nations University, 1984, 221–52.

Krepon M. and Shoenberger S., *Anti-Satellite Weapons, Deterrence and Sino-American Space Relations: A Report*. Washington, DC: Stimson Center, 2013.

Lawrence Livermore National Laboratory, 'Adapting to a Changing Weapons Program', *Science & Technology Review*, (January 2001). https://www.llnl.gov/archives/1980s/brilliant-pebbles Accessed 23 November 2025.

Lukiv J., 'US says Russia Likely Launched Anti-Satellite Weapon', *BBC News*, (22 May 2024). https://www.bbc.com/news/articles/cq55ww5j7e2o Accessed 23 November 2025.

Mao W., Pang T., Guo Z., et al., 'Analysis of the Research Progress of Electromagnetic Railgun Based on CiteSpace', *IEEE Access*, 20 (2017). https://www.researchgate.net/publication/377071631_Analysis_of_the_Research_Progress_of_Electromagnetic_Railgun_Based_on_CiteSpace Accessed 23 November 2025.

Melzer N., *Interpretative Guidance on the Notion of Direct Participation in Hostilities Under International Humanitarian Law*. Geneva: ICRC, 2009.

NATO, 'NATO Centres of Excellence: Enhancing Capabilities, Interoperability, and Education', (18 July 2024). https://www.act.nato.int/article/nato-centres-of-excellence/#:~:text=Although%20not%20officially%20part%20of,%2C%20exercise%2C%20and%20evaluation%3B%20and Accessed 23 November 2025.

NATO, 'NATO Space Centre'. https://shape.nato.int/about/aco-capabilities2/nato-space-centre Accessed 30 November 2025.

NATO, 'NATO's Approach to Space', (21 March 2024). https://www.nato.int/cps/en/natohq/topics_175419.htm Accessed 23 November 2025.

New Space Economy, 'The Secret Soviet Quest for Space-Based Weapons', (27 May 2024). https://newspaceeconomy.ca/2024/05/27/the-secret-soviet-quest-for-space-based-weapons/ Accessed 23 November 2025.

The New York Times, 'Reagan Urges Antimissile Effort to Defend U.S.' (24 March 1983), A1.

The New York Times, 'General Describes Soviet Laser Threat', (24 October 1987), Section 1, 62.

Ocotec Oy, 'What Does an EMP (Electromagnetic Pulse) Do?', (19 June 2024). https://ocotec.fi/en/what-does-an-emp-electromagnetic-pulse-do/ Accessed 28 November 2025.

Paperkamp L. and Bolder P., 'The Space Domain and Russia-Ukraine War', in Maaerten Rothman, et al., eds. *Reflections on Russia-Ukraine War*. Leiden: Leiden University Press, 2024, 257–74.

Parmentola J. and Tipsis K., 'Particle Beam Weapons', *Scientific American*, 240 (1979), 51–65.

Pierini V., 'The Involvement of the Private Sector in the Militarisation of Outer Space and the Liability Problem', *Finabel: The European Land Force Commanders Organization*, (April 2025), 5–6. https://finabel.org/the-involvement-of-the-private-sector-in-the-militarisation-of-outer-space-and-the-liability-problem/ Accessed 23 November 2025.

Pobjie E., 'The Threat from Outer Space: Russia Tests Kinetic DA-ASAT Weapon', *Just Security*, (23 November 2021). https://www.justsecurity.org/79320/the-threat-from-outer-space-russia-tests-kinetic-da-asat-weapon/ Accessed 23 November 2025.

Podvig P. and Zhang H., *Russian and Chinese Responses to US Military Plans in Space*. Cambridge, MA: American Academy of Arts and Sciences, 2008.

Preston B., Johnson D. J., Edwards S. J. A., et al., *Space Weapons Earth Wars*. Washington, DC: RAND Corporation, 2002.

Raju N., 'A Proposal for a Ban on Destructive Anti-Satellite Testing: A Role for the European Union?', *Non-Proliferation and Disarmament Papers*, 74 (2021), 1–16. https://www.sipri.org/publications/2021/eu-non-proliferation-and-disarmament-papers/proposal-ban-destructive-anti-satellite-testing-role-european-union Accessed 23 November 2025.

Ruhle H., 'Gorbachev's Star Wars', *NATO Review*, 33 (1985), 29–38.

Satam P., 'Scrapped by US Navy after $500M Investment, China "Succeeds" in Electromagnetic Railgun-Fired "Smart Shell" – Reports', *The EurAsian Times*, (9 February 2024). https://www.eurasiantimes.com/railgun-fired-smart-dream-shell-but-us-spent-500/ Accessed 23 November 2025.

Singh K., 'Russia's Resurgence in Space: Anti-Satellite Capabilities and Tests', *Centre for Air Power Studies*, (26 February 2024). https://capsindia.org/russias-resurgence-in-space-anti-satellite-capabilities-tests/ Accessed 23 November 2025.

Siouris G. M., *Missile Guidance and Control Systems*. New York: Springer, 2004.

Skynet Coverage, https://web.archive.org/web/20140516082649/http://www.satcom-airbusds.com/products-solutions/government-satcom/products-systems/bandwidth/skynet-5-x-band/#satellite-coverage-skynet-5-x-band Accessed 23 November 2025.

Smith M., 'Satellite and Missile ASAT Systems and Potential Verification Problems Associated with the Existing Soviet Systems', in Jasani B., ed., *Space Weapons: The Arms Control Dilemma*. Stockholm: SIPRI, 1984, 83–91.

Smithsonian: National Air and Space Museum, https://timeandnavigation.si.edu/satellite-navigation/who-uses-satellite-navigation/military-applications Accessed 23 November 2025.

The Space Review, https://www.thespacereview.com/article/4121/1 Accessed 23 November 2025.

Stefanova A., 'The Role of Geodesy in Military Operations: Historical Developments and Modern Use', *Security and Defence*, 1 (2025), 213–22. https://journals.indexcopernicus.com/api/file/viewByFileId/2412110#:~:text=Military%20engineers%20used%20geodetic%20data,of%20military%20strategy%20and%20tactics Accessed 28 November 2025.

Stewart M., 'The Strategic Defence Initiative in Retrospect: The Past, Present and Future of Missile Defense', *US Department of State*, (April 2023). https://www.state.gov/the-strategic-defense-initiative-in-retrospect-the-past-present-and-future-of-missile-defense/ Accessed 23 November 2025.

Stone M. and Mason J., 'Trump Selects $175 Billion Golden Dome Defense Shield Design, Appoints Leader', *Reuters*, (21 May 2025). https://www.reuters.com/world/us/trump-make-golden-dome-announcement-tuesday-us-official-says-2025-05-20/ Accessed 23 November 2025.

Stone M. and Taylor M., 'Musk's SpaceX Is Forerunner to Build Trump's Golden Dome Missile Shield', *Reuters*, (17 April 2025). https://www.reuters.com/business/aerospace-defense/musks-spacex-is-frontrunner-build-trumps-golden-dome-missile-shield-2025-04-17/ Accessed 23 November 2025.

Stonis D., 'Ambiguities in Space Law as Path Towards Weaponisation of Space: The Case of the Outer Space Treaty', *Copernicus Political and Legal Studies*, 1 (2022), 74–84.

Stroikos D., 'Still Lost in Space? Understanding China and India's Anti-Satellite Tests Through an Eclectic Approach', *International Journal of Space Politics and Policy*, 21 (2023), 181–205. https://www.tandfonline.com/doi/full/10.1080/14777622.2023.2277253 Accessed 23 November 2025.

Swope C., Bingen K. A., Young M., et al., *Space Threat Assessment 2024*. Washington, DC: Center for Strategic and International Studies, 2024. https://www.csis.org/analysis/space-threat-assessment-2024 Accessed 23 November 2025.

TASS, 'Russian Anti-Satellite System'. https://www.russianspaceweb.com/naryad.html Accessed 23 November 2025.

United States Space Force, https://www.spaceforce.mil/About-Us/Fact-Sheets/Fact-Sheet-Display/Article/2197774/defense-support-program-satellites/ Accessed 23 November 2025.

U.S. Department of Defense, *Report to the Congress on Strategic Defense Initiative*, April 1987, VI-D-1.

U.S. General Accounting Office, 'Statement by Donald E. Day, Senior Associate Director, Mission Analysis and Systems Acquisition Division, before the Subcommittee on Strategic and Theatre Nuclear Forces, Committee of Armed Services, United States Senate on Space-Based Lasers', (16 March 1982). https://www.gao.gov/assets/117803.pdf Accessed 23 November 2025.

U.S. Government Accountability Office, 'Science and Tech Spotlight: Directed Energy Weapons: Fact Sheet', (25 May 2023). https://www.gao.gov/assets/gao-23-106717.pdf Accessed 23 November 2025.

4 Legal examination of outer space military activities

After examining the current, planned, and expected military activities of various states and other actors in outer space, a question arises: Where does international law stand regarding the militarisation of outer space? As seen earlier, numerous norms already exist within current international law that directly and indirectly address military activities in outer space and on celestial bodies. Now, it remains to determine which military activities outlined in the previous chapter are permitted and which are prohibited. This chapter attempts to do so in light of the legal framework discussed in Chapters 1 and 2.

Lawfulness of military satellites

In the previous chapter, a thorough survey of satellites used for various military purposes was conducted. It is important to emphasise that their use today represents a significant military activity in outer space. The term 'military satellites' as used here includes all those satellites that, at present, serve military purposes, namely, reconnaissance, early warning, ocean surveillance, communication, meteorology, navigation, and geodesy. These military uses of outer space are considered 'passive' military missions.[1] Apart from early warning, other purposes also serve civilian applications. It is likely that, in the future, satellites may be placed in outer space for other military purposes, such as parts of a space weapons system or as weapons platforms. Evaluating the legality of such satellites would require different criteria. It is also likely that, in the future, satellites forming essential components of space weapons systems could be used alongside conventional military satellites, so that all satellites involved in the space weapons system may form an integrated, unified space weapons system. Since this remains a hypothetical scenario, the present analysis is confined to conventional military satellites.

1 Martin Feinrider, *Proceedings of the American Society of International Law*, 79th Annual Meeting, (1985), 235.

DOI: 10.4324/9781003754428-5

Satellite reconnaissance: Is it espionage?

Although most state espionage and reconnaissance share a common goal – the collection of information about an adversary's military affairs – there are some differences between the two processes. Espionage is typically carried out by individuals who enter another country's territory, either legally or illegally. These days, hackers who infiltrate computer systems can do so from within or outside the territory. Reconnaissance usually involves using electronic or optical devices to collect data. It can be carried out from an adversary's territorial airspace or from outside it. Bin Cheng describes these two types as 'penetrative' and 'peripheral' reconnaissance.[2] However, the present author prefers to refer to them as 'territorial' and 'extraterritorial' reconnaissance. As will be demonstrated later, extraterritorial reconnaissance can now be conducted from a location far removed from the 'periphery' of the state being observed.[3]

Territorial reconnaissance always infringes on the sovereignty of the observed state. It breaches international law and, like espionage, is regarded as a crime under that state's domestic law. The mere presence of reconnaissance devices, equipment, or vehicles in the state's territorial airspace, but not necessarily used, is sufficient to violate sovereignty. Extraterritorial reconnaissance may be carried out from the territory of the conducting state, a friendly state with its consent, international airspace, the high seas, or from *terra nullius*. Similarly, it can also be conducted from outer space. Such reconnaissance does not violate the territorial sovereignty of the observed state. Therefore, regardless of its potential security implications, it does not constitute a breach of international law. At most, it can be considered an unfriendly or hostile act by the observed state. It is not the act of collecting information that determines legality, but rather the location from which it is gathered.[4]

In the early days of space exploration, some states viewed satellite reconnaissance as espionage, thereby categorising all forms of intelligence gathering under a single heading. For instance, in 1960, the Soviet Union warned that forceful action could be taken against new methods of *espionage* and that such measures would be fully justified by existing international law, including the United Nations Charter.[5] At that time, the Soviet Union regarded satellite reconnaissance as equivalent to aerial espionage. It warned that, to protect its security against any encroachment from outer space, such satellites would be

2 See generally, Bin Cheng, 'United Nations and Outer Space', *Current Legal Problems*, 14 (1961), 262–72.

3 Here the term 'observed' is used to indicate the state regarding whom the data are collected.

4 Umesh Kadam, 'Espionage with Modern Technology: The Legal Implications', *National Law School Journal*, 7 (1995), 51–2.

5 G. P. Zukov, 'Space Espionage Plans and International Law', *International Affairs*, 6 (1960), 57. Emphasis added.

'paralysed and rebuffed'.[6] It was also claimed that such an encroachment violates the legal regime of airspace as outlined by the Chicago Convention of 1944.[7] Such claims were definitively and persuasively refuted by McMahon in 1962, with convincing reasoning that remains valid today.[8] He observes that a reconnaissance satellite located outside a country's sovereign airspace and taking photographs of that country's secret military facilities would not constitute a violation of international law.[9]

The practice of states involved in space exploration, supported by *opinio juris*, has established a rule that collecting militarily sensitive information about an adversary using a reconnaissance satellite does not constitute a violation of international law. Alternatively, interpreting Article IV of the Outer Space Treaty in light of the subsequent practice of its state parties leads to the same conclusion. Currently, all space-faring nations, including the United States and Russia, endorse this view, either explicitly or implicitly.

Other military satellites

The points made about reconnaissance satellites also apply to other conventional military satellites discussed earlier in this chapter. Reconnaissance satellites were emphasised because early debates in space exploration focused on them, and reconnaissance is purely a military activity, unlike other functions like communication or navigation, which also serve civilian purposes. Therefore, satellites used for activities such as early warning, ocean surveillance, communication, meteorology, navigation, and geodesy for military purposes do not breach international law, since they are in outer space, beyond the national jurisdiction of any state other than the country that launched them. Consequently, states that are probably affected by these satellite activities have no legal grounds to claim a violation of their national sovereignty or other international law norms.

Prohibited and permitted weapons in outer space

As observed earlier, some states are seriously developing various types of weapons for deployment and use in and from outer space. Since existing space law addresses certain military activities in outer space, including the deployment of specific categories of weapons, it is essential to evaluate each weapon under development from a legal perspective.

6 Ibid., 53.

7 Ibid., 55–6.

8 J. F. McMahon, 'Legal Aspects of Outer Space', *British Yearbook of International Law*, 38 (1962), 367.

9 Ibid.

Kinetic energy weapons

Kinetic energy weapons are intended to target and eliminate specific objects. They do not depend on nuclear energy for their destructive method. Therefore, they are not prohibited under international law, whether terrestrial or space-based. Similarly, electromagnetic railguns that do not rely on nuclear energy and are not expected to cause widespread satellite destruction are not prohibited by law.

Killer satellites

As noted earlier, the killer satellites that approach their target satellite and explode nearby, thereby damaging or destroying the target, rely on chemical non-nuclear explosives. Their targets are expected to be individual satellites selected for destruction. They are neither nuclear nor able to cause mass destruction. Therefore, they do not fall within the scope of weapons prohibited in outer space.

Directed energy weapons

As noted in the previous chapter, some states are exploring the possibility of developing X-ray lasers for anti-satellite and anti-ballistic missile applications that require a nuclear detonation. Since these lasers depend on nuclear detonation, some commentators argue that X-ray lasers are nuclear weapons within the meaning of Article IV of the Outer Space Treaty.[10] It may be recalled that, based on the interpretation used in this study, only nuclear weapons that cause mass destruction are covered by Article IV. Therefore, nuclear weapons can be categorised into two types:

1. Those designed to release a large amount of uncontrolled energy to cause indiscriminate destruction of property and/or harm to human beings on a massive scale, or in other words, to cause mass destruction.
2. Those that utilise nuclear energy for their operational mechanism without releasing uncontrolled energy. The energy produced by such devices can be controlled, directed, and selectively utilised to destroy specific targets without causing mass devastation.

Those that fall into category 1. are typical nuclear weapons, which are devices designed to release energy explosively through nuclear fission, nuclear fusion, or a combination of both processes.[11]

10 D. Goedhuis, 'Some Observations on the Attitude of West European Governments to the Development of Defensive Weapons in Outer Space', *Journal of Space Law*, 15 (1987), 107.

11 *Britannica*, https://www.britannica.com/technology/nuclear-weapon Accessed 24 November 2025.

The author believes that nuclear-pumped X-ray lasers belong to category 2. since they are not weapons of mass destruction. Therefore, they will be excluded from the scope of Article IV of the Outer Space Treaty. Technically, they might be nuclear weapons, but not of the kind envisaged by Article IV of the Outer Space Treaty. It is argued that lasers are nuclear weapons under the Outer Space Treaty because the basic atomic physics underlying such weapons involves the emission of destructive energy automatically produced by fission or fusion processes.[12] However, the focus in Article IV is on destructive capacity rather than the processes involved in the operational mechanism. Their use will not lead to the catastrophic consequences usually linked with weapons of mass destruction. Lasers, including those produced by X-rays and other types, are not weapons of mass destruction because their purpose is to destroy a hostile satellite or a ballistic missile. It could be argued that using a laser weapon against a satellite vital to the state could have 'catastrophic consequences' for that state and therefore should be considered a weapon of mass destruction. While it is true that such a laser could threaten the security or strategic interests of the affected state, this does not constitute a physically devastating consequence. The term 'mass destruction' refers to the physical loss of property and lives. Consequently, it is now widely accepted that laser weapons under development do not cause destruction comparable to atomic bombs.[13]

What is said about laser weapons also applies to particle beam weapons. The available information about directed energy weapons so far indicates that they are unlikely to be weapons of mass destruction. However, if a space weapon of mass destruction based on laser technology is developed in the future, it would naturally fall under the category of prohibited weapons as outlined in the Outer Space Treaty.

Electromagnetic pulse weapons

As mentioned earlier in the previous chapter, electromagnetic pulse (EMP) weapons rely on a nuclear detonation at high altitude. An electromagnetic pulse is thought to be able to destroy satellites that enter or happen to be within the highly charged area created by the nuclear explosion. Such destruction would be indiscriminate. Technically, there is no distinction between a terrestrial nuclear weapon and an electromagnetic pulse weapon. Since it can destroy any satellite within the charged field, it can be regarded as a weapon of mass destruction. Although the intensity of an electromagnetic pulse weapon

12 See generally, Rex Zedalis and Catherine Wade, 'Anti-Satellite Weapons and the Outer Space Treaty of 1967', *California Western International Law Journal*, 8 (1976), 454–62.

13 Rudiger Wolfrum, 'The Problems of Limitation and Prohibition of Military Use of Outer Space', *Zeitschrift Fur Auslandisches Offentiches Recht Und Volkerrecht*, 44 (1984), 794.

may be comparatively lower than that of conventional nuclear warheads, this is not a decisive factor. The ability to destroy all objects indiscriminately is crucial in defining a weapon's mass destruction potential. Consequently, it is categorised as a weapon prohibited in outer space.

Another legal basis for classifying it as a prohibited weapon is the Partial Nuclear Test Ban Treaty of 1963. It explicitly prohibits, among other things, a nuclear explosion in outer space if such an explosion results in radioactive debris outside the territorial limits of the state conducting the explosion. It is quite probable that a nuclear detonation intended to create an electromagnetic pulse in outer space will generate radioactive debris.

Radio-frequency weapons

These weapons are believed to be in use at present. Their typical targets are GNSS, GPS, and communication satellites. Since they operate by emitting a radio signal generated from electrical energy directed at a hostile satellite to interfere with its function, they do not fall under the weapons prohibited by Article IV of the Outer Space Treaty. To date, there is no evidence that all satellites within the radio signal's spectrum are rendered dysfunctional by such weapons. If that were the case, they could be classified as weapons of mass destruction and therefore banned under Article IV.

Anti-satellite weapons and space debris

Certain types of anti-satellite weapons discussed so far, notably kinetic energy weapons such as killer satellites and direct-ascent ASAT weapons, would produce significant space debris. Currently, there is no explicit prohibition on the generation of space debris in existing space treaties. However, if debris from kinetic energy weapons continues to damage and/or destroy satellites other than the target satellite, presumably belonging to other countries, then such weapons might be regarded as indiscriminate weapons prohibited under customary international humanitarian law.[14]

Deployment of weapons in outer space

From the foregoing analysis, it is clear that, apart from electromagnetic pulse weapons, all other weapons currently being researched, developed, and used for outer space applications do not fall under the category of prohibited weapons, such as weapons of mass destruction, as specified in Article IV of the

14 ICRC, 'Customary International Humanitarian Law Database', Rule 71. https://ihl-databases.icrc.org/en/customary-ihl/v1/rule71 Accessed 24 November 2025.

Outer Space Treaty. Therefore, their presence in outer space would not violate any current legal obligation. This aligns with the established principle of international law: What is not prohibited is permitted. Regarding the deployment of weapons in outer space, it has been argued that a strict interpretation of Article IV of the Outer Space Treaty prohibits the placement or stationing of objects carrying nuclear or mass-destruction weapons, but does not prohibit the placement or stationing of such weapons themselves.[15] Therefore, it is further argued that if the object is the weapon itself, it might not be prohibited.[16] It would be a gross misinterpretation of both the purpose of Article IV and the spirit of the Outer Space Treaty to interpret it in such a circuitous manner. Article IV not only bans placing objects containing the specified weapons into orbit but also forbids stationing such weapons in outer space by any other means. This latter requirement is quite broad, prohibiting the orbiting of specific weapons or, for that matter, placing such weapons in outer space in any manner imaginable. Today, it is plausible to develop a weapon of mass destruction and place it in orbit around the Earth. With rapid technological advances in weaponry, it becomes very hard to distinguish between a weapon and an object or satellite equipped with a weapon. For example, consider a killer satellite. Is it a weapon or a satellite? It could be both at the same time. Therefore, it would be incorrect to draw a strict line between a weapon and an object that carries a weapon, as this would undermine the purpose and aim of the provision.

Deployment of weapons on celestial bodies

The combined effect of Article IV of the Outer Space Treaty and Article 3 of the Moon Treaty is complete demilitarisation of celestial bodies.[17] The provisions of these two articles are clear, unambiguous, and unequivocal. References in these articles to the use of celestial bodies solely for peaceful purposes, along with a strict prohibition on establishing military bases, installations, and fortifications, have not only de-weaponised the celestial bodies but also fully demilitarised them. Outlining specific military activities prohibited on celestial bodies is illustrative but not comprehensive.

Stephen Gorove expressed doubt about the complete de-weaponisation of celestial bodies. Referring to the prohibition in Article 3(2) of the Moon Treaty on the threat or use of force or threat of a hostile act on celestial bodies, he wondered if they had been totally de-weaponised, why it was necessary to prohibit such threat or use of force or threat of a hostile act on them.[18]

15 Dana St. James, 'The Legality of Antisatellites', *Boston College International and Comparative Law Review*, 3 (1980), 478. Emphasis added.

16 Ibid.

17 Here the term 'celestial bodies' includes the moon.

18 *Report of the Sixty-First Conference of the International Law Association*, (1984), 364.

In the author's view, such a prohibition does not imply that weapons can be stationed on celestial bodies. Such a prohibition also reinforces the obligation to prevent the militarisation of celestial bodies. Furthermore, it cannot be ignored that states may develop weapons capable of causing damage on celestial bodies that could be located on Earth's surface, in the airspace, on the high seas, or in outer space.

Deployment of terrestrial space weapons

The term 'terrestrial space weapons' might seem like an oxymoron, but in this context, it refers to weapons that can be deployed on land, in the air, or at sea, designed to target objects in outer space. Earlier, we noted that some countries do not classify Earth-to-space weapons as 'space weapons'. However, for this work, any device capable of causing damage or destruction in outer space or on celestial bodies is classified as a space weapon. As discussed in Chapter 3, the current plans to develop ground-based anti-satellite weapons and ballistic missile defence systems fall into this category. Electromagnetic railguns, directed energy weapons, and radio-frequency weapons are designed for terrestrial deployment. Some of these would need components such as sensors, reflectors, mirrors, and similar devices to be placed in outer space.

The existing space treaties do not contain any provisions that would restrict states' rights to develop terrestrial space weapons, including their components, for deployment in outer space, excluding celestial bodies. Since the early years of space law development, restrictions on the development of terrestrial space weapons have never been on the agenda of relevant United Nations bodies, as such restrictions would not have been acceptable to any state. The limited provisions in space treaties governing military activities apply solely to outer space and celestial bodies.

The law of the sea could govern sea-based terrestrial space weapons. The United Nations Convention on the Law of the Sea of 1982 specifically states that the 'high seas shall be reserved for peaceful purposes'.[19] This provision does not prohibit military activities on the high seas, such as the passage of warships, reconnaissance, weapons testing, and naval exercises. Currently, most seafaring states utilise the high seas for these military activities. It might be argued that this has become part of customary international law. The obligation to use the high seas for peaceful purposes is generally understood as prohibiting only acts of aggression on the high seas, rather than covering other military actions, such as disarmament.[20] Therefore, merely deploying a directed energy weapons system on a warship and sailing it on the high

19 Article 88 of the Convention.

20 R. R. Churchill and A. V. Lowe, *The Law of the Sea* (Manchester: Manchester University Press, 1983), 276.

seas would not breach the aforementioned provision. Warships equipped with space weapons will also have the right of innocent passage through the territorial waters of other states if exercised in accordance with the provisions of the Law of the Sea Convention of 1982.[21]

Deploying space weapons on aircraft in flight is almost the same as deploying weapons on land, provided the aircraft is flying within national airspace. It can also operate in international airspace above the high seas because, under the law of the sea, the freedom of the high seas includes the freedom of overflight, which is granted to both civilian and military aircraft. Therefore, the points made previously about military activities in the high seas also apply to aircraft carrying space weapons and flying in international airspace. This is significant because certain states developing space weapons are contemplating the aerial deployment of these weapons.

Lawfulness of use of weapons in and from outer space and on celestial bodies

The relevance of laws concerning the use of force and self-defence in outer space has already been discussed in Chapter 3. However, given the significant technological advances made so far and those currently underway in space weaponry, traditional concepts of 'use of force' and 'threat of force' need to be revisited. The types of space weapons that some states are developing can be classified into two categories: (a) Those designed to destroy a target using kinetic or directed energy physically, and (b) those intended to disable an object without physical destruction by using electronic means, such as radiofrequency waves. In the first category, the effect of the 'force' or damage can be observed physically. These are primarily developed for anti-satellite, anti-ballistic missile, and anti-terrestrial purposes. In the second category, the effect of 'force' is not physically observable. However, in both cases, the level of impact could be similar. For example, disrupting a satellite's telecommunications without visible damage could be just as critical and dangerous for the security of the affected state as physically attacking it. Another example could be deliberately changing a satellite's trajectory or orbit by any means to render it useless for its owner.

In the context of space activities, it can be argued that deliberately interfering with the normal operation of a space object should be considered equivalent to 'use of force' against the state operating it. It is commonly understood that when a space object is launched into outer space, various parameters are predefined by the launching state, such as its intended flight path or trajectory, duration in orbit, apogee and perigee, inclination, and most importantly, the

21 The relevant provisions are to be found in Articles 17 to 26 of the Convention.

function it is designed to perform. A deliberate interference with its function and operation to disable it may take one or more of the following forms:

1. Disrupting or blocking the communication system or facilities;
2. Changing flight trajectory or orbital parameters;
3. Damaging electronic components;
4. Communicating misleading instructions;
5. Physical damage or destruction; and
6. Capture.

These are just a few examples showing how interference with a space object's normal operation can make it useless. There might be alternative ways to achieve similar results, especially given ongoing technological advancements. If interfering with a space object's normal functioning is regarded as the use of force in outer space, then means of such interference can be classified as space weapons. Various kinetic and non-kinetic devices described in Chapter 3 should be regarded as space weapons. Their use might result in an armed attack, depending on the severity of the consequences, and could also be considered an act of aggression.

Therefore, whenever space weapons are used against their intended targets, such use shall be governed by international law on the use of force, particularly Article 2(4) and Article 51 of the United Nations Charter.

Self-defence in outer space

Earlier in Chapter 2, the debate over the limits and scope of the right of self-defence in international law was discussed. As noted there, the debate centres on whether current international law permits anticipatory self-defence to justify pre-emptive military action. If, for argument's sake, the existence of such a right is accepted, tensions and hostility between space-faring nations pose significant challenges. A state, wrongly believing that a hostile actor is about to launch an attack, might strike an adversary's military satellite as a preventive measure. The targeted state might view this as an act of aggression and retaliate with hostilities on Earth or towards objects in outer space. Claims and counter-claims will make it very difficult to determine which state is legitimately using military force. Without an impartial and objective third party to verify the facts, the situation could escalate into a full-scale war between the parties. This section examines the different challenges of exercising the right of self-defence in space warfare.

Preventive action against military satellites

The numerous satellites that serve various military functions, such as early warning, reconnaissance, communication, and navigation, could be regarded as military targets whose destruction might provide a distinct military advantage if carried out as a preventive measure. As previously mentioned, such satellites and their activities are generally not considered to violate international law, especially space law. In many cases, these satellites could pose a serious threat to the national security of certain states. However, their mere deployment and use cannot be classified as 'threat or use of force', nor as an act of aggression or armed attack. Nonetheless, during the early stages of space exploration, there was significant uncertainty and confusion about the implications of using such satellites, particularly reconnaissance satellites. This observation highlights these concerns:

> A strict interpretation of Article 51 of the Charter might give rise to serious theoretical objections in the case of intelligence satellites not directly constituting an armed attack. The strategic role of surveillance from outer space, however, might turn the activity of the intelligence satellites into an act of aggression . . . . Thus, in the given case the interception of an attack from outer space begins with paralyzing the equipment providing the necessary data thereto. *The fact that so far no such measures have been taken, does not amount to a waiver on the part of the states to make use of this possibility at a later date.*[22]

At that time, the Soviet Union asserted it could use military force against an intelligence satellite in accordance with international law and the United Nations Charter, presumably based on Article 51.[23] Anticipatory preventive action by a state against other nations' intelligence satellites was deemed lawful if it threatened the state's security, based on a broad interpretation of Article 51 of the Charter.[24] Such action might also be justified by reference to the *Caroline* formula. Preventive action against a surveillance satellite was also justified 'if the space vehicle were engaged in conduct unreasonably dangerous to the existence of the inspecting state [sic]'.[25] These views were founded on the premise that the presence of a reconnaissance satellite in outer space, gathering information about another state, constitutes an act of aggression against that state. Consequently, the affected state may respond with the use of force against such a satellite in line with Article 51 of the Charter. Such views are no longer valid, as the legitimacy granted to military satellites through widespread state practice accompanied by *opinio juris* has led to the development of a customary space law norm to that effect. The mere presence of these satellites is no longer considered an act of aggression or armed attack, and

22 Gal, *Space Law*, 185. Emphasis added.

23 Zukov, 'Space Espionage Plans', 53.

24 D. Goedhuis, 'Some Trends in the Political and Legal Thinking on the Conquest of Space', *Netherlands International Law Review*, 9 (1962), 131.

25 Carl Christol, *International Law of Outer Space* (Newport: U.S. Naval War College, 1966), 346.

therefore does not justify the use of force against them in self-defence. However, the scenario could change if tensions between states escalate to the point where both have mobilised ground forces or taken other measures indicating an imminent military confrontation. One state might opt to neutralise an adversary's military satellite to weaken its capacity through anticipatory self-defence. In such cases, the justification for using force against the satellite would arise from the imminent threat of armed attack rather than merely from the presence of a hostile military satellite in outer space. Furthermore, once hostilities between states escalate into an international armed conflict, the opposing side's military satellites would become legitimate military targets under the norms of international humanitarian law.

Preventive action against space weapons

The issue of preventive action in outer space is further complicated by plans to station weapons systems there. Unlike reconnaissance or other military satellites, these could be explicitly weapons designed to carry out attacks on hostile objects in space and on Earth's surface. Could their presence in outer space be considered an imminent threat to the security of the state against which they are most likely to be used?

The right of a state to enhance the capacity and preparedness of its military forces is a core feature of sovereignty. Clearly, this right must be exercised within the boundaries set by international law. Apart from territorial jurisdiction, military preparedness can also occur outside a state's territory in two situations: First, within the territory of another friendly state with its consent; and second, in international spaces. States regularly operate military aircraft equipped with missiles in international airspace and sail warships armed with various military hardware in international waters, including submarines. Similarly, military activities in outer space would be lawful sovereign actions unless a specific international law norm explicitly prohibits them. For example, consider Article IV of the Outer Space Treaty. As long as no weapons are stationed on celestial bodies and no weapons of mass destruction are placed or stationed in outer space, deploying other types of weapons there would be lawful military activity. There is no reason why states should not adopt military measures that align with technological advancements.[26] The mere presence of non-prohibited weapons in outer space does not justify preventive forcible action against them, even if they threaten the security of another state. However, military escalation between two states may permit one of them to use military force against space weapons systems as a pre-emptive action if the threat of an imminent armed

26 Harry Almond, 'Military Activities in Outer Space: The Emerging Law', *Proceedings of the Twenty-Fourth Colloquium on the Law of Outer Space*, (1981), 150.

attack can be demonstrated. Some commentators claim that a state may justifiably use force to cease military activities in outer space that violate international law, such as the deployment of weapons of mass destruction in outer space.[27] However, as noted earlier, according to the International Law Commission's 2001 draft Articles on State Responsibility for Internationally Wrongful Acts, only non-forcible countermeasures may be taken by a state in response to an internationally wrongful act by another state to stop the violation.[28]

Self-defence in outer space and the proportionality rule

Forcible measures taken by a state in self-defence must be proportionate to the threat posed by the attack to repel it and protect its interests. Although Article 51 does not specify the extent of force permitted in self-defence, there is a universal understanding that defensive actions under Article 51, as well as under customary international law, should be proportionate to the force used in the attack. A reference in the *Caroline* formula to 'nothing unreasonable or excessive; since the act, justified by the necessity of self-defence, must be limited by that necessity, and kept clearly within it' illustrates how firmly the principle of proportionality of defensive measures is embedded in customary international law.[29] In land, naval, and air warfare, it may not be difficult to assess the severity or scale of an armed attack to determine the appropriate proportionate response in self-defence. Even if assessing the severity of an armed attack proves difficult, countermeasures can still be taken as long as the original attack continues.

Regarding self-defence in outer space, the need for proportionality becomes more significant, as assessing it presents particular challenges. This issue is also related to the question of whether defensive measures should be restricted to the area of the armed attack. It was once thought to be so. Notably, Fawcett's view is especially striking.

> [T]he use of force in self-defence must be controlled by the principle of proportionality. It must correspond with the attack in the kind of force employed; it must be proportionate to the attack in the degree of force used; and it must be reasonably *co-extensive in time and place* with the attack.[30]

27 Rex J. Zedalis, 'On the Lawfulness of Forceful Remedies for Violation of Arms Control Agreements: "Star Wars" and Other Glimpses at the Future', *New York University Journal of International Law and Politics*, 18 (1985), 80–2, 107. A similar view was expressed even before the Outer Space Treaty came into force. See A. S. Becker, 'The Military Implications of Space', *Report of the Symposium on Current Problems in Space Law*, British Institute of International and Comparative Law, (1966), 76.

28 Commentary on Draft Article 1. United Nations, *Yearbook of the International Law Commission*, 2001, vol. II, Part Two, 32–4.

29 D. J. Harris, *Cases and Materials on International Law* (London, Sweet & Maxwell, 1983), 655–6.

30 Fawcett, *International Law*, 39. Emphasis added.

In today's context, such insistence on co-terminousness could undermine the right of self-defence. For instance, if a state carries out a series of attacks against terrestrial objects of another state, the latter might choose to neutralise a satellite of the former that is crucial to launching the original attacks. It might prove more effective than an attack by way of self-defence against the terrestrial objects of the aggressor state. Since military satellites have proven very useful in coordinating the terrestrial use of force, space assets, such as those used for military purposes, as well as terrestrial assets, such as command, control, and communication stations, may also be considered potential targets for countermeasures. Writing in 1966, Brownlie, prima facie, agreed that countermeasures should be confined to the source of the attack, but admitted that, in a situation like the one described above, effective defensive measures can only be taken by destroying control mechanisms in the state of origin or even in its military pacts' allies.[31] He also noted that in cases of vicious and repeated attacks on ships and aircraft, defensive measures could be taken against the territorial bases of the vessels and aircraft conducting the attacks.[32]

As discussed earlier in Chapter 3, the space weapon systems being considered by some states aim to establish or station their components in various locations: In outer space, in airspace, on the high seas, or on land within the territory of the state or its allies in military pacts. All such objects and facilities may be considered potential targets for countermeasures if the situation requires it. Since the early 1970s, a trend has emerged favouring the justification of defensive measures outside the initial attack zone, particularly in the context of outer space hostilities.[33] The location of countermeasures also depends on the technological abilities of the attacked state. It can also be argued that the requirement for countermeasures to be co-terminous was never an absolute rule. Since the early days of space exploration, the United States has maintained that even if an attack originates from outer space, defensive measures can be taken elsewhere.[34] Once the requirement of co-terminousness is dispensed with, a state subjected to a terrestrial aggressive armed attack is free to take countermeasures against space objects of the aggressor state.

One challenge in implementing countermeasures against space assets is assessing the proportionality of the response. Most probably, only the launching state is aware of the precise capabilities of the space object it has launched. The United Nations Register of space objects might not contain all information about the purpose and usefulness of the object for the launching state. Space-faring nations tend to be secretive about information related to their

31 Brownlie, 'Maintenance of Peace', 24.
32 Ibid., 23.
33 John Kish, *The Law of International Spaces* (Leiden: A.W. Sijthoff, 1973), 183.
34 Statement of Mr. Loftus Becker, Legal Adviser, made before the Special Senate Committee on Space and Aeronautics, *Department of State Bulletin*, 38 (1958), 965.

space missions. Additionally, many space objects serve dual purposes – both military and civilian. Countermeasures against a satellite used for military communications could have disastrous consequences for the civilian population of the launching state. Apart from the strategic setback, the attacked state will also incur substantial financial losses from the countermeasure. Overall, the proportionality requirement is most likely to pose practical challenges for compliance when applied to space assets.

The Outer Space Treaty and self-defence

The right of a state to self-defence in and from outer space is unaffected by the Outer Space Treaty. In the early days of space law development, there was some uncertainty about the implications of the obligation to use outer space for 'peaceful' purposes and its impact on the exercise of the right of self-defence. This has already been discussed in Chapter 1. Regarding the exercise of the right of self-defence in outer space following the adoption of the Outer Space Treaty, Carl Christol noted that this right remains unaffected because the use of force in self-defence is not considered an act of aggression. Furthermore, non-aggressive activities are permitted in outer space because they are considered 'peaceful' in nature.[35] In contrast, Manfred Lachs believed that 'peaceful purposes' are indicative of measures of a non-military nature.[36] However, he acknowledged that this could raise problems for exercising the inherent right of self-defence and therefore suggested that self-defence should be treated as a notable exception to the rule.[37]

Today, the interpretative debate surrounding the term 'peaceful purposes' has little practical relevance. As discussed in Chapter 3, outer space is regularly used for various military purposes. There is extensive state practice to support this. Furthermore, it is now well-established that international law, including the Charter of the United Nations, applies to outer space. The clear conclusion from this is that the right of self-defence can be exercised in outer space, except where space treaties prohibit certain military activities. Therefore, defensive weapons cannot be stationed on celestial bodies, and defensive mass-destruction weapons are not permitted in outer space.

Self-defence on celestial bodies

As previously discussed in Chapter 1, unlike outer space itself, the moon and other celestial bodies have been completely demilitarised. The establishment

35 Carl Christol, *Modern International Law of Outer Space* (New York: Pergamon Press, 1982), 37.

36 Manfred Lachs, *The Law of Outer Space: An Experience in Contemporary Law Making* (Leiden: A.W. Sijthof, 1972), 106.

37 Ibid., 107.

of military bases, installations, and fortifications on them is strictly forbidden. At the same time, any threat, use of force, or other hostile acts against them are also forbidden. This raises the question: Can the right of self-defence be exercised on and from celestial bodies? Let us recall paragraph 2 of Article 3 of the Moon Treaty that addresses demilitarisation.

> Any threat or use of force or any other hostile act or threat of hostile act on the moon is prohibited. It is likewise prohibited to use the moon in order to commit any such act or to engage in any such threat in relation to the Earth, the moon, spacecraft, the personnel of spacecraft or man-made space objects.

All states may access celestial bodies for scientific exploration by establishing stations or installations there.[38] In the event of any act of aggression against such a state facility, the question arises whether the affected state may use force by way of self-defence on celestial bodies. A strict interpretation of the quoted paragraph 2 of Article 3 would prevent this. Although it is based on Article 2, paragraph 4, of the United Nations Charter, the former does not allow any exceptions, unlike the latter, which permits the use of force in accordance with the purposes of the Charter. However, since Article 2 of the Moon Treaty requires States Parties to conduct activities on celestial bodies in accordance with international law, particularly the United Nations Charter, it seems that States Parties are entitled to the rights guaranteed under the Charter, including the right of self-defence.

If an act of aggression is committed against an installation by another state from its own installation on a celestial body, military force may be used with impunity from outside the celestial body against the military facility that committed the act of aggression. It is also possible to argue that military force used in this manner is defensive and, therefore, it is not 'hostile' within the meaning of Article 3(2) of the Moon Treaty. If force is used against an installation from outside the celestial body, then defensive action may be taken against the source of the force or elsewhere except on the celestial body.

All things considered, the issue of using force on celestial bodies remains distant due to technological challenges in establishing stations or installations there. Furthermore, at present, states have no plans to develop weapons for use on celestial bodies. All ongoing research and development efforts are focused on capabilities to destroy objects in or from low Earth orbit. The debate about self-defence on celestial bodies remains speculative and hypothetical for now.

38 Articles 8 and 9 of the Moon Treaty.

Armed conflict in outer space and international humanitarian law

Earlier, we observed that international humanitarian law would apply to situations involving the use of force in or from outer space. Now we must consider the implications of this law for the military activities currently underway and those planned for the near future by various states. Although technically, the entire body of international humanitarian law would apply to outer space, some norms are more relevant to an armed conflict in outer space, while others are entirely irrelevant. To begin with, a reference to Article 36 of the Additional Protocol I of 1977 to the Geneva Conventions would be appropriate:

> In the study, development, acquisition or adoption of a new weapon, means or method of warfare, a High Contracting Party is under an obligation to determine whether its employment would, in some or all circumstances, be prohibited by this Protocol or by any other rule of international law applicable to the High Contracting Party.

Many leading space powers are not parties to the Additional Protocol I. The obligation in Article 36 does not appear to have acquired the status of customary law. Even for states that are parties to the Protocol, the obligation is only to consider in good faith whether new weapons are compatible with international humanitarian law. So far, there is no indication that states developing space weapons have explicitly evaluated whether their weapons programmes adhere to international humanitarian law requirements. One fundamental rule of humanitarian law concerning weapons is that the use of means and methods of warfare likely to cause superfluous injury or unnecessary suffering is prohibited.[39] This rule is irrelevant for space weapons because most of the weapons under development are anti-object rather than anti-personnel. In the context of space weapons, the rule prohibiting the use of indiscriminate weapons would be more relevant.[40]

International humanitarian law protects civilians, civilian populations, and civilian objects. To ensure this protection, parties involved in armed conflicts must distinguish between civilians and combatants, as well as between civilian objects and military targets. Means and methods of warfare that cannot differentiate between civilian and military targets are deemed indiscriminate and are prohibited. Since most of the space weapons under consideration are anti-object weapons, we can focus primarily on the distinction between civilian objects and military targets. Article 52(2) of Additional Protocol I defines

39 ICRC, 'Customary International Humanitarian Law Database', Rule 70. https://ihl-databases.icrc.org/en/customary-ihl/v1 Accessed 24 November 2025.

40 Ibid., Rule 71.

military objectives as those that make an effective contribution to military action and whose complete or partial destruction, capture, or neutralisation offers a distinct military advantage. Using this criterion, it can be concluded that all military satellites discussed in Chapter 3 fall within this category. Similarly, all space weapons and components of space weapon systems located in outer space, airspace, high seas, or on land may be included in this category. All other space objects should be considered civilian objects and must not be targeted. The main challenge arises with space objects that serve both military and civilian functions. The vast majority of satellites launched into space serve dual functions. Such dual-use objects lose civilian protection and may be lawfully targeted during armed conflict if they satisfy the military objective test established in Article 52(2).

Another related norm is the principle of proportionality. The notion of proportionality in the law of self-defence and international humanitarian law has different connotations. In international humanitarian law, this principle prohibits attacks that are likely to cause incidental loss of civilian life, injury to civilians, or damage to civilian objects that would be excessive in comparison with the concrete and direct military advantage anticipated.[41] Most space weapons considered by states are not indiscriminate. They are designed to target specific objects – whether satellites in space, ballistic missiles in transit, or terrestrial targets. Therefore, these weapons are unlikely to cause extensive damage to civilian objects. However, dual-use space objects present a challenge. The impact of neutralising or destroying a dual-use satellite on civilian life must be considered when assessing the proportionality of the attack. Therefore, attacking a dual-use satellite that qualifies as a military target would be unlawful if it is expected to cause incidental harm to civilians that is disproportionate to the military advantage obtained. For example, neutralising satellites that are crucial for healthcare systems could have long-term, widespread consequences, even if they perform some less critical military functions. Therefore, even if a space object loses its protection due to its dual functions, any attack must still adhere to the principles and rules of proportionality and precaution, and ensure compliance with international humanitarian law norms that grant protection to medical, humanitarian, and other assets.[42]

The only space weapon that appears to be indiscriminate is the electromagnetic pulse weapon, which can destroy all space objects within the electrically charged field generated by an atomic explosion. As previously noted, it appears to be a weapon of mass destruction and therefore not in conformity with

41 Article 51 (5) (b) of Additional Protocol I of 1977 and ICRC, 'Customary', Rule 14.

42 ICRC, 'Statement Delivered to the United Nations Open-Ended Working Group on the Prevention of an Arms Race in Outer Space in All Its Aspects', (5 August 2025). https://www.icrc.org/en/statement/weaponization-of-space-not-inevitable Accessed 24 November 2025.

the Outer Space Treaty. Being inherently indiscriminate, it would also violate international humanitarian law. All weapons of mass destruction are inherently indiscriminate by nature.

The use of military personnel and objects for purely peaceful purposes is permitted by both the Outer Space Treaty and the Moon Treaty. When personnel and objects participate in non-military activities, they are entitled to the protection granted to individual civilians and civilian objects under international humanitarian law. The test is functional. As mentioned earlier in the context of the Astronauts Agreement, the Soviet Union, Romania, and Bulgaria insisted during negotiations that if a space object was not launched in accordance with the Declaration of Legal Principles, astronauts landing in another state could be considered spies or prisoners of war, rather than 'envoys of mankind' as the Astronauts Agreement intended.[43] These countries also reaffirmed that, in the event of detention, they would be treated in accordance with the requirements of international humanitarian law. Given the limited number of manned space missions so far, such questions have not yet arisen. The whole matter hinges on how the Declaration of Legal Principles is interpreted, especially its mention of 'peaceful purposes' as previously discussed.

The issue of civilian protection may come up in relation to space-to-Earth weapons. When such weapons are employed against terrestrial targets from outer space, all necessary precautions for protecting individual civilians and the civilian population,, as mandated by international humanitarian law, must be observed. This also includes the obligation to ensure that the principle of proportionality is respected.

Modification of the outer space environment for military purposes

From a technological standpoint, altering Earth's natural environment, including its airspace and outer space, is feasible. In most cases, it will result in far-reaching adverse consequences. If such modifications are carried out for hostile military reasons, they would raise numerous legal and ethical issues. Such manipulation is incompatible with the ENMOD Convention. As noted earlier, Article I of this Convention prohibits the modification of the environment for military or other hostile purposes. The Convention explicitly forbids the modification of the outer space environment.[44]

Another weapon that could involve modifying the natural environment of outer space is the electromagnetic pulse weapon. If a nuclear detonation produces an electromagnetic pulse, it would immediately affect satellites within

43 *Supra*, Chapter 1, at 17.
44 Article II of the Convention.

its range. Simultaneously, it would create a high-radiation environment that would accelerate the degradation of satellite components over time for all unshielded satellites in the affected orbit.[45] Nevertheless, a nuclear detonation that produces a highly charged field would constitute a modification of the outer space environment. Furthermore, a nuclear detonation could also cause extensive, long-lasting, and severe effects on the environment, which the ENMOD Convention categorically prohibits.[46]

Testing of weapons in outer space and on celestial bodies

While the Outer Space Treaty remains silent on testing weapons in outer space, it explicitly prohibits testing any weapon on celestial bodies. Article IV of the Treaty and Article 3(4) of the Moon Treaty clearly state that testing weapons on celestial bodies is forbidden. Understandably, during negotiations on the Outer Space Treaty, states did not want to eliminate the possibility of testing new space weapons. Therefore, all weapons that comply with the space treaties may be lawfully tested in outer space. However, certain weapons may be subject to restrictions under the legal regulations governing them. For example, in the case of nuclear weapons, the relevant treaties on testing would apply and may impose restrictions. As previously noted, the PTBT prohibits nuclear weapon test explosions or any other explosions, *inter alia*, in outer space if such explosions cause radioactive debris to be present outside the territorial limits of the state conducting the explosion.[47] It is worth noting that an electromagnetic pulse weapon involves a nuclear explosion in outer space. Its testing, as well as actual use involving a nuclear explosion in outer space, is explicitly prohibited by the PTBT.

Non-delimitation of airspace and outer space: Implications for military activities

Few issues in space law have generated more controversy than the absence of a legal definition of outer space and the resulting lack of a clear boundary between airspace and outer space. The concept of 'outer space' has defied definition since the dawn of the space age, mainly due to policy considerations rather than legal criteria. The leading space powers struggle to agree on a boundary between airspace and outer space, primarily because such a boundary could affect military activities in outer space.

45 Todd Harrison, Kaitlyn Johnson and Makena Young, 'Space Defences Defined', *Defence Against the Dark Art in Space: A Report* (Washington, DC: Centre for Strategic and International Studies, 2021), Chapter 3.

46 Article I (1) of the Convention.

47 Article I (1) (a) and (b) of the Treaty.

There are two perspectives on delimitation. According to one, spatial delimitation is unnecessary, and the legality or illegality of an activity should be assessed by its nature rather than its location. This is known as the 'functional' approach. Advocates of the second perspective, the 'spatial' approach, argue that the lawfulness of an activity depends on its location, making spatial delimitation a prerequisite for determining its legality. The functionalists are not uniform in their approach. The only common denominator amongst them is that spatial delimitation is either not needed at all or not needed at present. Bin Cheng has summarised the functionalist trends as follows:

(a) Spatial delimitation is not required at all:
   (i) Astronautics can be regulated by reference solely to the nature of the activities;
   (ii) Astronautics can be regulated by reference solely to the nature of the activities and the nature of space objects;

(b) Spatial delimitation is not required at present, and astronautics can be adequately regulated at present by either (a) (i) or (a) (ii) above.[48]

The functional approach was vigorously defended by McDougal and Lasswell as early as 1963. Their assertion was:

> It may . . . be emphasised that in principle we do not favour any boundaries in super-incumbent regions unless it can be demonstrated that such boundaries promote inclusive interest. The possible temporary boundary we suggest, and any other solution which would artificially limit man's freedom of exploration, navigation and communication should be considered as no more than a transitional agreement, reflecting not so much long-term general community interests as short term, transient, particularistic interests which do not express the true needs of the space age but are rather a relic of the past.[49]

There are several inherent weaknesses in the functionalist approach. It introduces significant ambiguity and uncertainty into space exploration. Countries involved in space activities may interpret the location of their space objects differently. Lack of clear delimitation could lead to a reduction in airspace sovereignty. The United States has consistently supported functionalism. In April 1979, the United States delegate argued in the Legal Subcommittee of

48 Bin Cheng, 'The Legal Regime of Air Space and Outer Space: The Boundary Problem, Functionalism Versus Spatialism – Major Premises', *Annals of Air and Space Law*, 5 (1980), 323.

49 Myres McDougal and Harold D. Lasswell, *Law and Public Order in Outer Space* (New Haven: Yale University Press, 1963), 359.

COPUOS that the boundary between air space and outer space is unnecessary because most states are unable to monitor such an altitude frontier; that the relevant legal, scientific, technical, and political factors have not been thoroughly examined; and, most importantly, that establishing a boundary could hinder and even suppress future space exploration.[50] He was replying to a proposal submitted by the Soviet Union in March 1979, in which it suggested the delimitation of airspace from outer space:

1. The region above 100 (110) kilometres from the sea level is outer space.
2. The boundary between air space and outer space shall be subject to agreement among States and shall subsequently be established by a treaty at an altitude not exceeding 100 (110) kilometres above sea level.
3. Space objects of States shall retain the right to fly over the territory of other States at altitudes lower than 100 (110) kilometres above sea level for the purpose of reaching orbit or returning to Earth in the territory of the launching State.[51]

The issue of defining outer space and its delimitation was included in the agenda of the Legal Subcommittee of the COPUOS for the first time in 1967.[52] Since then, disagreements over the definition of outer space have continued in its discussions. During deliberations in the Legal Subcommittee in June 2024, many delegations expressed the view that delimitation remains an important topic and that more work should be done on it.[53] During the June 2025 meeting of the Legal Subcommittee, the differences in approach between states persisted.[54] During this meeting, a view was expressed that, while some states have adopted or proposed definitions of outer space for purposes such as regulatory compliance, administrative clarity, or tax laws, this should not be considered as emerging state practice that might eventually lead to a customary norm for defining outer space.[55] Thus, the disagreement over this issue has persisted for nearly 60 years. Some space powers, particularly the United States, have long been concerned that delimitation will limit their freedom in outer space, especially their ability to conduct military activities such as satellite reconnaissance.

The absence of a clear boundary between airspace and outer space has significant implications for military operations in outer space, as discussed in the following.

50 UN Doc. A/AC.105/C.2/SR.316, 2–3.
51 UN Doc. A/AC.105/C.2/L.121.
52 UN Doc. A/6804, 5.
53 UN Doc. A/79/20, 25.
54 UN Doc. A/AC.105/1362, 15.
55 Ibid.

Right of transit

A key practical issue arising from non-delimitation is whether states have the right to transit the airspace of other states with their space objects, including military ones, to access and return from outer space. Currently, international law does not recognise such a right. However, since there is no clear boundary between airspace and outer space, space powers gain advantages in their approach to and departure from outer space.[56] Basing their argument on the permissibility or non-permissibility of space activities, the functionalists claim that airspace sovereignty is irrelevant for space flights. The core of the functionalist argument is that once an activity is deemed permissible, a space object engaged in that activity has the right to transit the airspace of other states. Cheng has convincingly argued that such a claim lacks legal foundation, especially as it breaches the principle of state sovereignty.[57] He has demonstrated that if such a transit is permitted for a state's space activities, the sovereignty of other states' airspace begins and ends at sea level, or it ceases to exist.[58]

When the United States launched the Space Shuttle programme in the early 1970s, it revived the debate over delimitation in the Soviet Union.[59] The United States was reluctant to accept a boundary due to concerns about its adverse effect on the transit of space objects. As previously mentioned, the Soviet Union was willing to agree to delimitation at 100/110 km, on the condition that space objects of states shall 'retain' the right to reach orbit or return to Earth. This is equivalent to asserting that states already possess such a right, and acceptance of the proposed formula would serve a declaratory or confirming purpose. While this Soviet proposal appeared to favour spatial delimitation, it is fundamentally very similar to the functionalist approach. To address the complex issue of transit rights, some space lawyers considered drawing parallels with the law of other international spaces, especially the law of the sea. J. E. S. Fawcett proposed that, to enable access to outer space, a right of innocent passage through the airspace should be established via a special agreement if a boundary is recognised.[60] He further clarified that the notion of 'innocent' would include at least registering the features of the spacecraft, its flight components, the purpose of the flight, and so on, with the United Nations; adhering to conditions necessary for safe navigation; and ensuring no prejudice to the good order or security of the underlying state.[61] Although we notice similarities among various international spaces, as they

56 Cheng, 'The Legal Status of Outer Space', 96.
57 Ibid., 97.
58 Ibid.
59 Gorove, *Studies in Space Law*, 44.
60 Fawcett, *International Law*, 24.
61 Ibid.

are viewed as the global or cosmic commons, significant fundamental differences remain between outer space and other international spaces, making direct comparisons challenging. Most states would probably deny granting a right of innocent transit because they do not have the means to effectively monitor the space frontier and verify the purpose of missions, unlike the innocent passage of ships through territorial waters.

Weapons in outer space and delimitation

The development of space weapons and the proposal to deploy them in outer space intensify the problem of delimitation. Countries developing space weapons insist that anti-satellite and anti-ballistic missile systems are for defensive, non-aggressive use and are therefore not prohibited by space law. They also assert that these are 'peaceful' weapons. It is worth noting that functionalists advocate for conducting all so-called 'peaceful' activities in outer space without establishing a specific spatial boundary. If that is the case, countries might deploy space weapons on satellites orbiting at any altitude they find convenient and strategically advantageous, asserting they are operating in outer space. Others may oppose this view, arguing that the satellite is orbiting within their airspace, not in outer space. Such states might view this as a breach of their airspace sovereignty and could respond with force to neutralise the threat. This type of confrontation in outer space could considerably endanger international peace and security.

Terrestrial directed energy weapons being developed for anti-satellite or anti-ballistic missile purposes are expected to project a charged beam at their targets. Such a beam might traverse the airspace of another state. These beams could represent a significant hazard to aircraft in flight. On this ground, the subjacent states may object to the traversal of charged beams through their airspace. Additionally, they may claim that traversing such beams constitutes a violation of their airspace sovereignty.

Use of force, self-defence, and delimitation

The mere presence of permitted weapons in outer space cannot justify preventive forcible action against them, even if they threaten another state's security. However, this presumes the deployment of weapons or their components in outer space rather than within the airspace of other states. If the boundary between airspace and outer space is not clearly defined, a state might consider the presence of a space object carrying weapons or their components as an intrusion into its airspace, amounting to an armed attack and an act of aggression, thereby justifying forcible measures based on the right of self-defence against such a space object. Even if such weapons are not used, the territorial state may still use force against them, asserting a right to anticipatory self-defence against an imminent threat of attack. Although the threat might not be imminent, the mere presence of a hostile weapon within its airspace could provide a strong justification for the use of force. These situations can be avoided by establishing a clear boundary between airspace and outer space.

Delimitation as a preventive measure

The previous discussion demonstrates that, now more than ever, clearly defining the boundaries between airspace and outer space is crucial. Amid rising attention to space weaponisation, defining spatial boundaries is essential for establishing order and security in outer space. In the early days of space exploration, the lack of a clear boundary was understandable because of the limited number of missions and the few space-faring nations. Today, as more states seek to participate in various military activities in outer space, it is crucial to ensure they exercise their rights with proper respect for the lawful interests of other states, thereby preventing friction and maintaining international peace and security. The absence of a clear boundary provides ample opportunity to ignore the sovereign rights and interests of underlying states with impunity.

Concluding remarks

From the previous analysis of the legality of various military activities in outer space and on celestial bodies, it is clear that some are strictly prohibited, such as establishing military bases, fortifications, and installations on celestial bodies; others are considered acceptable or even lawful, like satellite reconnaissance; and some are not explicitly addressed but are presumed to be permitted, such as current plans for stationing non-mass-destruction weapons in outer space. This shows that the existing legal framework governing outer space is insufficient to prevent the weaponisation of space. Unchecked weaponisation of space will undoubtedly threaten international peace and security. This requires further development of the legal framework. The international community recognises these risks and is working to develop the legal framework further, but, as is often the case in international law-making related to peace, security, arms control, and similar issues, the process is painfully slow. Significant differences persist among the leading space powers. Nevertheless, various proposals have been put forward in the past and continue to be proposed. In the following chapter, the different proposals and positions held by leading space powers concerning the militarisation of space are discussed.

References

Almond H., 'Military Activities in Outer Space: The Emerging Law', *Proceedings of the Twenty-Fourth Colloquium on the Law of Outer Space*, (1981), 149–57.

Becker A. S., 'The Military Implications of Space', *Report of the Symposium on Current Problems in Space Law*, British Institute of International and Comparative Law, (1966), 71–105.

Britannica, https://www.britannica.com/technology/nuclear-weapon Accessed 24 November 2025.

Brownlie I., 'The Maintenance of Peace and Security in Outer Space', *British Yearbook of International Law*, 40 (1964), 1–31.

Cheng B., 'The Legal Regime of Air Space and Outer Space: The Boundary Problem, Functionalism Versus Spatialism – Major Premises', *Annals of Air and Space Law*, 5 (1980), 323–38.

Cheng B., 'United Nations and Outer Space', *Current Legal Problems*, 14 (1961), 262–72.

Christol C., *International Law of Outer Space*. Newport: U.S. Naval War College, 1966.

Christol C., *Modern International Law of Outer Space*. New York: Pergamon Press, 1982.

Churchill R. R. and Lowe A. V., *The Law of the Sea*. Manchester: Manchester University Press, 1983.

Fawcett J. E. S., *International Law and Uses of Outer Space*. Manchester: Manchester University Press, 1968.

Feinrider M., *Proceedings of the Annual Meeting of the American Society of International Law*, 79th Annual Meeting, (1985), 235.

Gal G., *Space Law*. Leiden: A.W. Sijthoff, 1969.

Goedhuis D., 'Some Observations on the Attitude of West European Governments to the Development of Defensive Weapons in Outer Space', *Journal of Space Law*, 15 (1987), 101–18.

Goedhuis D., 'Some Trends in the Political and Legal Thinking on the Conquest of Space', *Netherlands International Law Review*, 9 (1962), 113–36.

Gorove S., *Report of the Sixty-first Conference of the International Law Association*, (1984), 363–5.

Gorove S., *Studies in Space Law: Its Challenges and Prospects*. Leiden: A.W. Sijthoff, 1977.

Harris D. J., *Cases and Materials on International Law*. London: Sweet & Maxwell, 1983.

Harrison T., Johnson K. and Young M., 'Space Defences Defined', *Defence Against the Dark Art in Space: A Report*. Washington, DC: Centre for Strategic and International Studies, 2021.

ICRC, 'CustomaryInternational Humanitarian Law Database', Rule 70. https://ihl-databases.icrc.org/en/customary-ihl/v1 Accessed 24 November 2025.

ICRC, 'Customary International Humanitarian Law Database', Rule 71. https://ihl-databases.icrc.org/en/customary-ihl/v1/rule71 Accessed 24 November 2025.

ICRC, 'Statement Delivered to the United Nations Open-Ended Working Group on the Prevention of an Arms Race in Outer Space in All Its Aspects', (5 August 2025). https://www.icrc.org/en/statement/weaponization-of-space-not-inevitable Accessed 24 November 2025.

Kadam U., 'Espionage with Modern Technology: The Legal Implications', *National Law School Journal*, 7 (1995), 51–2.

Kish J., *The Law of International Spaces*. Leiden: A.W. Sijthoff, 1973.
Lachs M., *The Law of Outer Space: An Experience in Contemporary Law Making*. Leiden: A.W. Sijthof, 1972.
McDougal M. and Lasswell H. D., *Law and Public Order in Outer Space*. New Haven: Yale University Press, 1963.
McMahon J. F., 'Legal Aspects of Outer Space', *British Yearbook of International Law*, 38 (1962), 339–71.
St. James D., 'The Legality of Antisatellites', *Boston College International and Comparative Law Review*, 3 (1980), 467–94.
UN Doc. A/79/20.
UN Doc. A/6804.
UN Doc. A/AC.105/1362.
UN Doc. A/AC.105/C.2/L.121.
UN Doc. A/AC.105/C.2/SR.316.
United Nations, *Yearbook of the International Law Commission*, 2001, vol. II, Part Two.
U.S. Department of State Bulletin, 38 (1958).
Wolfrum R., 'The Problems of Limitation and Prohibition of Military Use of Outer Space', *Zeitschrift Fur Auslandisches Offentiches Recht Und Volkerrecht*, 44 (1984), 784–805.
Zedalis R., 'On the Lawfulness of Forceful Remedies for Violation of Arms Control Agreements: "Star Wars" and Other Glimpses at the Future', *New York University Journal of International Law and Politics*, 18 (1985), 73–167.
Zedalis R. and Wade C., 'Anti-Satellite Weapons and the Outer Space Treaty of 1967', *California Western International Law Journal*, 8 (1976), 454–62.
Zukov G. P., 'Space Espionage Plans and International Law', *International Affairs*, 6 (1960), 53–7.

5 Legal regulation of military activities in outer space

Proposals and perspectives

The previous discussion indicates that numerous states have been actively working to weaponise outer space, alongside other military operations, since the early 1960s. Apart from a few provisions in space treaties and specific norms of international law, the militarisation of outer space remains largely unregulated. Major actors are actively advancing space weaponisation programmes. These developments undoubtedly constitute a serious threat to global peace and security. At the same time, many other states, as well as the United Nations, are deeply concerned about the extension of an arms race to outer space.

Although the issue of preventing an arms race in outer space has been on the international community's agenda since the early 1980s, progress has been painfully slow. It can be attributed to two main factors. Initially, during the Cold War, no significant progress was achieved due to the tense environment, which influenced relations between the two leading space powers. Later, the momentum behind space weaponisation, driven by President Ronald Reagan's Strategic Defence Initiative of the early 1980s, waned after the end of the Cold War. Consequently, preventing an arms race in outer space was not a priority in the 1990s. However, after a lull of over ten years, the momentum of space weaponisation revived in the early 2000s. It also revived the international debate on the de-weaponisation of outer space. Therefore, to understand the current position, it is necessary to review the proposals put forward so far and the positions held by leading space powers and their allies. It is also essential to consider what the United Nations has achieved thus far in promoting the peaceful use of outer space. At the same time, it is equally important to review proposals from other entities, academic bodies, and individual experts for maintaining peace and order in outer space. This is discussed in the present chapter.

Developments in the United Nations

Before examining the outcomes of the debate and discussion on military activities in outer space within the United Nations, a brief mention of a controversy regarding the appropriate forum for this matter is desirable. At the

DOI: 10.4324/9781003754428-6

twenty-fourth session of the COPUOS in 1981, delegates from Austria, Brazil, Canada, Chile, Egypt, India, Romania, and Sweden stated that COPUOS would be a suitable forum for addressing the issue of preventing an arms race in outer space.[1] However, the United States strongly opposed this proposal, asserting that preventing an arms race in outer space is closely connected to the complex issue of terrestrial disarmament and arms control, and that it goes beyond the expertise and mandate of the COPUOS.[2] It has also been noted that the principle of consensus, on which the COPUOS operates, was likely to hinder progress in this regard.[3] The Soviet Union and other Eastern European states believed that COPUOS was the appropriate forum, as the militarisation of outer space poses a serious threat to peaceful cooperation.[4] Given the growing support for the United States' position, during its thirty-sixth session in 1981, the General Assembly requested the Committee on Disarmament to include, in its 1982 agenda, the issue of arms control in outer space under the title 'Prevention of an arms race in outer space'.[5] However, UN members were divided on the nature of the threat posed by space weaponisation and the best way to respond to it.[6] This division was evident in two resolutions on space weaponisation.[7] One resolution sponsored by Western European and other states urged the Committee on Disarmament to focus on negotiating 'an effective and verifiable agreement to prohibit anti-satellite systems'.[8] In contrast, in December 1981, the second resolution, sponsored by Eastern European and other states, aimed to have the Committee focus on negotiating a treaty prohibiting the stationing of any weapons in outer space.[9] The differences of opinion among these groups of states persisted in the CD year after year. Thus, since the early 1980s, discussions on proposals to demilitarise outer space have taken place in various United Nations forums without any positive outcome.

Since the early 2000s, China and Russia have spearheaded efforts in the CD to address the challenges posed by the weaponisation of outer space. China submitted a Working Paper to the Conference on Disarmament in February 2000.[10] It included various elements for a new international legal instrument

1 UN Doc. A/AC.105/PV. 220.
2 Ibid.
3 *Report of the Twenty-Seventh Session of the COPUOS*, Vienna, (12–21 June 1984), partially reproduced in *The UN Chronicle*, 10/11 (1984), 54.
4 Ibid.
5 *The United Nations Disarmament Yearbook*, 7 (1982), 370.
6 Paul Meyer, 'The CD and PAROS: A Short History', *CD Discussion Series*, UNIDIR, (April 2011), 1.
7 Ibid., 2.
8 UN Docs. A/RES/36/97.
9 UN Docs. A/RES/36/99.
10 UN Doc. CD/1606.

to address the challenges posed by the prospects of space weaponisation.[11] In 2002, Russia decided to collaborate with China on developing proposals for a future treaty on space weaponisation. In June 2002, they jointly submitted a Working Paper that outlined potential elements of the future treaty.[12] Following this initiative, in February 2008, they jointly submitted a draft treaty on space weaponisation titled 'Treaty on Prevention of Placement of Weapons in Outer Space and of the Threat or Use of Force Against Outer Space Objects' (PPWT).[13] The United States and its allies raised several objections to the draft. In August 2008, the United States submitted a paper to the Conference on Disarmament outlining its objections.[14] Later, in June 2014, China and Russia submitted a revised draft of PPWT.[15] It largely follows the structure of the 2008 draft, with some notable alterations. Key features of the revised draft are summarised next:

1. The draft does not define 'outer space' and thus indirectly avoids the contentious issue of delimitation of airspace from outer space. The 2008 draft had foreseen delimitation at 100 km above sea level.
2. The draft excludes actions that cause temporary or reversible effects, such as those resulting from radio-frequency jamming and optical sensor dazzling, or the deliberate modification of another country's space object's orbit.
3. The definition of 'weapons in outer space' only covers space-to-space and space-to-Earth weapons, not Earth-to-space weapons. Hence, the draft, instead of defining 'space weapons', merely defines 'weapons in outer space'. A weapon is considered 'placed' in outer space if it orbits the Earth at least once, or follows a section of such an orbit before leaving it, or is permanently situated somewhere in outer space. Thus, it would include fractional orbital bombardment systems (FOBS) and, probably, some types of intercontinental ballistic missiles (ICBMs). In FOBS, the missiles enter low Earth orbit at an altitude of about 150 km before re-entering the airspace. ICBMs go to higher altitudes, from about 1200 km to 4500 km, before entering the airspace.
4. Although the prohibition on the use or threat of force in outer space may be seen as unnecessary given Article 2(4) of the United Nations Charter, the proposed draft aims to define what might constitute the use or threat of force against a space object. It clarifies that 'use of force' or the 'threat of force' includes any hostile actions against outer space objects, such as,

11 Ibid., 5.
12 UN Doc. CD/1679.
13 UN Doc. CD/1839.
14 UN Doc. CD/1847.
15 UN Doc. CD/1985.

among other things, actions aimed at destroying them, damaging them, temporarily or permanently disrupting their normal functioning, or deliberately changing their orbital parameters, or the threat of such actions. This formula encompasses all possible applications of various kinetic and non-kinetic space weapons based on different physical principles that are currently being considered by certain states, as discussed earlier in Chapter 3. The draft clarifies that the treaty should not be interpreted as hindering the right of self-defence under Article 51 of the United Nations Charter.

5. The fundamental obligation to refrain from deploying weapons in space is outlined in Article II of the draft.
6. The draft includes voluntary confidence-building measures. However, provisions for verifying compliance with the treaty are left to an additional protocol to be negotiated separately.
7. The draft encourages consultation in dispute resolution and recommends negotiation and cooperation to accomplish this. If the parties are unable to resolve their disputes through negotiations, the draft proposes referring the issue to an Executive Organisation. Once again, the specifics of such an organisation are left to an additional protocol to be negotiated separately.
8. The draft allows amendments to the treaty through a consensus of States Parties.

Many provisions of the draft treaty, as well as its fundamental premise, are unacceptable to the United States and other Western states. The United States presented its primary objections in a Note Verbale sent to the Conference on Disarmament in September 2014.[16] These are summarised in the following.

1. *Lack of verification mechanism:* There is no comprehensive verification regime to help monitor or verify the restrictions on the placement of weapons in space. The United States could not endorse an approach in which verification provisions were decided solely through subsequent negotiations on an additional protocol. Furthermore, the United States has argued that, with current technologies and/or collaborative measures, it is not feasible to verify an agreement banning space-based weapons reliably.
2. *Scope of the Treaty:* Typically, arms control treaties that ban the deployment of a certain class of weapon also bar the possession, testing, production, and stockpiling of such weapons to prevent a country from quickly breaking out of these treaties. The PPWT does not contain such prohibitions so that a Party could develop a readily deployable space-based weapons break-out capability.
3. *Terrestrial anti-satellite weapons:* The Treaty does not address the most urgent, current threat to outer space systems: Terrestrially-based

16 UN Doc. CD/1998.

anti-satellite weapon systems. There is no prohibition on the research, development, testing, production, storage, or deployment of terrestrially-based anti-satellite weapons; therefore, such capabilities could be used as a substitute for, and to perform the functions of, space-based weapons.

The differences of opinion between the United States and its allies on one side, and China, Russia, and their supporters on the other, continue to this day. The core issue is that the United States does not want any restrictions on its plans to develop and deploy anti-ballistic missile systems in outer space. In contrast, China and Russia do not want to abandon their terrestrial ASAT programmes. They are also worried about the potential to repurpose anti-ballistic missile systems for ASAT applications.

The Group of Governmental Experts on transparency and confidence-building measures in outer space activities, 2012–13

The Group of Governmental Experts (GGE) on TCBM in Outer Space Activities originated in the UN General Assembly's First Committee, which deals with security and disarmament issues.[17] In 2010, the United Nations General Assembly requested the Secretary-General to establish the GGE. It was set up in 2011. The GGE was formed primarily because of the deadlock in the Conference on Disarmament, which blocked meaningful discussions on preventing an arms race in outer space. In July 2013, the GGE submitted its final report, approved by consensus, to the UN Secretary-General.[18] The UN General Assembly endorsed it and urged UN Member States to voluntarily review and implement the proposed measures through relevant national mechanisms. In August 2016, the United States submitted a Note Verbale to the Conference on Disarmament regarding the implementation of the recommendations made by the GGE.[19] The Note elaborates on the TCBMs identified by the GGE that are relevant to the work of the Conference on Disarmament, the implementation of some of them by the United States, and considerations for the Conference on Disarmament on how to leverage the work of the GGE.

United Nations General Assembly resolutions on the non-first placement of weapons in outer space

Expressing deep concern about the potential for an arms race in outer space and the danger of outer space becoming a battlefield for military conflict, the

17 UN Doc. A/RES/65/68.
18 UN Doc. A/RES/68/189.
19 UN Doc. CD/2078.

United Nations General Assembly has been annually adopting a resolution on 'No first placement of weapons in outer space' since December 2014.[20] Such resolutions necessitate a political commitment from member states not to be the first to deploy weapons in outer space. As of December 2024, 35 states have made such commitments. Among the states with space weapons programmes, only the Russian Federation has made such a commitment.[21] However, Russia's ground-based ASAT weapons programme remains outside the scope of the commitment. Furthermore, the commitment does not include research, development, and possession of weapons that could be deployed in outer space, likely on short notice.

The Group of Governmental Experts on further practical measures for the prevention of an arms race in outer space, 2018–19

In 2017, the United Nations General Assembly requested that the Secretary-General establish a group of governmental experts to develop further practical measures to prevent an arms race in outer space. The group met in two two-week sessions, one in 2018 and another in 2019, to consider and make recommendations on key elements of an international legally binding instrument aimed at preventing an arms race in outer space, including, among other issues, the prevention of the placement of weapons in outer space.[22] Although the group reviewed several drafts of a substantive report, no consensus was reached on the final version.[23] Thus, the deadlock observed in the Conference on Disarmament was reflected in the proceedings of this GGE.

The UN General Assembly resolution calling for a moratorium on direct-ascent ASAT weapons tests

The United States announced a unilateral moratorium on direct-ascent ASAT weapons testing in April 2022. This sparked discussions within the United Nations Open-Ended Working Group on Reducing Space Threats through Norms, Rules, and Principles of Responsible Behaviours, which was established in December 2021.[24] Many states supported the adoption by the General Assembly of a resolution calling for a unilateral moratorium on direct-ascent ASAT

20 UN Doc. A/Res/79/20.

21 For the list of member states that have made a commitment, see UN Doc. A/Res/69/32.

22 United Nations Office for Disarmament Affairs, https://disarmament.unoda.org/topics/outer-space/paros-gge/#:~:text=In%20accordance%20with%20operative%20paragraph,ended%20intersessional%20informal%20consultative%20meeting%2C Accessed 25 November 2025.

23 Ibid.

24 *Infra*, p. 98.

weapons testing.[25] The resolution adopted in December 2022 has two goals: To prevent damage to the outer space environment caused by space debris and to curb the arms race in outer space.[26] It received 155 votes in favour, nine against, and nine abstentions. So far, 37 states have made unilateral declarations placing a moratorium on such tests. Among the states with direct-ascent ASAT capability, China, India, and Russia have not made any such declaration.

The Open-ended Working Group on reducing space threats through norms, rules, and principles of responsible behaviours

The General Assembly established the Open-ended Working Group on reducing space threats through norms, rules, and principles of responsible behaviour in December 2021. Between May 2022 and September 2023, it held four working sessions. Although the group discussed all aspects of the mandate entrusted to it, it failed to reach consensus.

The Group of Governmental Experts on further practical measures for the prevention of an arms race in outer space, 2023–24

In December 2022, the General Assembly decided to reconvene a group of governmental experts to reconsider and make recommendations on key elements of an international legally binding instrument on the prevention of an arms race in outer space, including, among other things, the prevention of the placement of weapons in outer space.[27] It also decided that the newly established GGE will operate by consensus, without prejudicing national positions in future negotiations. The final report of the GGE recognises that the discussions fostered a better understanding of issues related to preventing an arms race in outer space, as well as consideration of key elements on this matter, including, *inter alia*, the prevention of weapons deployment in outer space and potential aspects of relevant negotiations.[28]

United Nations Security Council, April–May 2024

In April 2024, the United States and Japan proposed a resolution in the Security Council to reaffirm the obligation of all States Parties to fully comply with the Outer Space Treaty, including prohibiting the placement of objects

25 UN Doc. A/RES/77/41.

26 Ibid., paragraph 2.

27 United Nations Office for Disarmament Affairs, https://meetings.unoda.org/gge-paros/group-of-governmental-experts-on-further-practical-measures-for-the-prevention-of-an-arms-race-in-outer-space-2023 Accessed 25 November 2025.

28 UN Doc. GE-PAROS/2024/CRP.4., paragraph 76.

carrying nuclear weapons or other weapons of mass destruction in orbit around Earth, installing such weapons on celestial bodies, or stationing them in outer space in any other manner. The resolution was not passed due to Russia's veto.[29] Later, in May 2024, Russia submitted a counter-proposal to reaffirm States' obligation not to place any kind of weapon in outer space – including those of mass destruction. It was defeated, securing only seven votes in favour (Algeria, Ecuador, China, Guyana, Mozambique, Russian Federation, Sierra Leone) and seven against (France, Japan, Malta, Republic of Korea, Slovenia, United Kingdom, United States), with one abstention (Switzerland).[30]

United Nations Open-ended Working Group on PAROS, 2024–2028

The General Assembly established this Open-ended Working Group (OEWG) in December 2024 to unify the two processes initiated by the Open-Ended Working Group of 2022–23 on Reducing Space Threats through norms, rules, and principles of responsible behaviour; and the work of the GGE on further practical measures for the prevention of an arms race in outer space.[31] As noted earlier, the OEWG of 2022–23 emphasised responsible behaviour and norms grounded in existing space law and international law, while the GGE focused on options for legally binding instruments to prohibit weapons and the use of force in space. Instead of maintaining these separate tracks, this new OEWG combines the two approaches into a single comprehensive process. It is required to meet twice a year for one-week sessions from 2025 to 2028. The first substantive meeting of this process took place in Geneva from 7 to 11 April 2025. As in previous instances, there was disagreement regarding both the agenda and the formal programme of work. The main disagreement centred on one question: Should the group's work proceed as a comprehensive discussion – as desired by the General Assembly – or be divided into separate tracks for legal and non-binding normative issues?

Developments outside the United Nations

Apart from the United Nations, some developments took place outside the organisation. These include a draft code, manuals, and suggestions from individual experts. These are discussed next.

29 United Nations, 'Security Council Fails to Adopt First-Ever Resolution on Arms Race in Outer Space, Due to Negative Vote by Russian Federation'. https://press.un.org/en/2024/sc15678.doc.htm Accessed 29 November 2025.

30 United Nations, 'For Second Time Since Late April Security Council Fails to Adopt First-Ever Resolution on Preventing Arms Race in Outer Space'. https://press.un.org/en/2024/sc15700.doc.htm Accessed 29 November 2025.

31 UN GA Res. A/79/512.

European Union's draft Code of Conduct for Outer Space Activities

To enhance the security, safety, and sustainability of activities in outer space, the European Union (EU) proposed a draft Code of Conduct for Outer Space Activities (draft Code) in response to United Nations General Assembly resolution 61/75 of 6 December 2006. This resolution urged member states to submit proposals on transparency and confidence-building measures within the framework of preventing an arms race in outer space. The EU conducted consultations with space-faring nations and produced a draft, which the Council of the European Union approved on 27 September 2010. Following international consultations, the draft Code was revised in 2013.[32]

The draft Code is a legally non-binding instrument that all States may accept voluntarily. It applies to all outer space activities carried out by a Subscribing State, whether alone or in partnership with other States, or by private entities under the jurisdiction of a Subscribing State. It also covers activities undertaken within the framework of international intergovernmental organisations. It aims to reinforce existing UN treaties and principles on outer space, as Subscribing States would commit to adhering to them and promote their universal acceptance. Additionally, it seeks to complement these principles by codifying new best practices that ensure the safety, security, and sustainability of space activities. Its scope goes far beyond space weaponisation, covering issues such as reducing space debris, avoiding collisions, and preventing conflicts over radio spectrum and orbital assignments to enhance sustainability, safety, and security. The draft Code also outlines various cooperation mechanisms, including notification of outer space activities, registration of space objects, provision of information on outer space activities, and a consultation mechanism.

The draft Code has elicited mixed reactions from the international community. Several emerging space-faring states voiced concerns about not being included in the process from the beginning.[33] Substantive issues with the draft Code concern its vague language and lack of clear definitions, the extent to which it is legally binding, worries that it could restrict freedoms for military and intelligence activities in space, and fears that it is 'arms control in disguise'.[34]

32 For the text, see *European Union External Action*, 'Diplomatic Service of the European Union'. https://www.eeas.europa.eu/sites/default/files/space_code_conduct_draft_vers_31-march-2014_en.pdf Accessed 25 November 2025.

33 Chris Johnson, 'Draft International Code of Conduct for Outer Space Activities: Fact Sheet', *Secure World Foundation*, (February 2014). https://swfound.org/media/166384/swf_draft_international_code_of_conduct_for_outer_space_activities_fact_sheet_february_2014.pdf Accessed 25 November 2025.

34 Ibid.

McGill Manual on International Law Applicable to Armed Conflict in Outer Space (MILAMOS)

Canada's McGill University has been a pioneer in the field of Air and Space Law since 1951, the year it established the Institute of Air and Space Law. In May 2016, it launched the manual on International Law Applicable to Military Uses of Outer Space (MILAMOS) Project to create a widely accepted manual clarifying the rules governing the military use of outer space by both States and non-State actors.[35] The project was proposed by a panel of international experts who participated in the Expert Roundtable on International Law Applicable to Military Activities in Outer Space, organised at McGill in 2015. The aim was to establish rules grounded in existing international law, including state practice, to regulate space activities during both peaceful times and periods of tension and armed conflict.[36] It was published in 2022. The Institute hopes that the manual will clarify the restrictions that international law places on the threat or use of force in outer space. Against the backdrop of rapidly evolving technologies and applications, it aims to examine which military uses and objects are lawful or outrightly prohibited in outer space.[37]

The manual has compiled existing international law relevant to military activities in outer space and added some new norms and elements. For example, the definitions of space activities in Rule 101 and military space activities in Rule 103 together cover not only activities in outer space but also terrestrial space activities. At appropriate places, the manual includes different aspects of transparency and confidence-building measures. For instance, Rule 122 on 'Provision of Information' expects states to inform 'the Secretary-General of the United Nations as well as the public and the international scientific community, to the greatest extent feasible and practicable, of the nature, conduct, locations, and results of their space activities, including military space activities'. Furthermore, Rule 125 on 'Registration of Space Objects with the United Nations' obliges States Parties to the Registration Convention to submit to the Secretary-General of the United Nations the information required by the Convention concerning space objects used for military space activities. Currently, states do not openly admit that objects registered with the United Nations were launched for a military mission. Rule 143 on 'Jamming and Spoofing of Communications' and Rule 144 on 'Interference with Telemetry, Tracking, and Command' effectively prohibit the use of radio-frequency weapons. Rule 146 on 'Weapons other than Weapons of Mass Destruction' implicitly recognises that such weapons can be stationed or placed in outer space. The only requirement is that they must be used in accordance with

35 McGill Institute of Air and Space Law, https://www.mcgill.ca/iasl/projects/mcgill-manual Accessed 25 November 2025.

36 Ibid.

37 Ibid.

international law, including the Charter of the United Nations and international space law. Rule 152 on 'Right of Self-Defence' enables a state to take defensive measures against space objects of an aggressor state, even if the attack originates from terrestrial sources.

Some experts claim that the MILAMOS standards are idealistic and, although effective in principle, unlikely to persuade leading nations to ratify or adhere to them.[38] There is some confusion in the first two chapters of the proposed rules, which do not clarify whether the rules outlined in the manual are comprehensive or intended only to supplement the existing rules of the Moon Treaty and other well-known sources of international space law.[39] It is observed that if the rules are interpreted as additions to existing international space law standards, Rule 128, which allows the use of natural resources from outer space, including the moon and other celestial bodies, for military space activities, would directly conflict with Article II of the Outer Space Treaty and Article 11(2) of the Moon Treaty, which prohibit such appropriation.[40] Rule 137 concerning countermeasures and Rule 138 regarding retorsion would – legally speaking, accurately – encourage military confrontation in outer space as well as on Earth's surface. Despite these shortcomings and limitations, the manual would encourage further debate and discussion, both within and outside the United Nations, on adopting a legally binding instrument acceptable, above all, to the leading space-faring nations.

The Woomera Manual

The development of the Woomera Manual on the International Law of Military Space Activities and Operations was led by the University of Adelaide, the University of Nebraska, the University of Exeter, and the University of New South Wales. The manual was published in 2024 after six years of research, discussions, consultations, and drafting. It involved approximately 50 key experts, executive consultants, associate experts, technical experts, peer reviewers, rapporteurs, and research assistants from around the world to research, discuss, and define the law applicable to military activities and operations in space.[41] A consultative meeting with states was held in June 2022 at The Hague, initiated by the Dutch Government and attended by approximately 24 space-faring nations. The manual was finalised after reviewing suggestions

38 Colsen Centner, 'One Small Step for Man, One Giant Problem for Mankind', *International and Comparative Law Review*, 32 (2022). https://international-and-comparative-law-review.law.miami.edu/one-small-step-for-man-one-giant-problem-for-mankind Accessed 25 November 2025.

39 Ibid.

40 Ibid.

41 Dale Stephens and Joanna Jarose, 'The Woomera Manual and Military Space Activities and Operations', *Lieber Institute, West Point*, (August 2024). https://lieber.westpoint.edu/woomera-manual-military-space-activities-operations/ Accessed 25 November 2025.

from the state representatives.[42] The sponsors of the project selected the name 'Woomera' to recognise the small town of Woomera in South Australia, where the country's first space missions took place, and to honour the Aboriginal word for an impressive spear-throwing device that enables greater accuracy and distance.[43]

The manual has compiled and succinctly restated the existing law derived from treaties and customary norms, including emerging state practice. It does not claim to establish or suggest new norms of international law governing military activities in outer space. Its focus is on general international law relevant to space activities, including the United Nations Charter, space law, and the law of armed conflict.

The manual details standards applicable to three particular situations. Part I describes standards applicable during peacetime, primarily based on existing space treaties and customary international law. For example, Rule 6, which concerns military intelligence gathering, reflects a customary norm widely supported by state practice and aligns with states' obligations under the Outer Space Treaty. Part II addresses military space activities during times of tensions and crises, primarily focusing on general international law, including the United Nations Charter. Part III deals explicitly with situations of armed conflict, focusing on international humanitarian law (IHL). Consequently, Rules 29 to 48 illustrate how IHL norms, developed through treaties and customary law, apply to and can be adapted for armed conflict scenarios in outer space. It may be recalled that the MILAMOS has not dealt with the application of IHL norms to armed hostilities in or from outer space.

Military space activities to gather intelligence from, to, and within space are not forbidden by Rule 6 of the manual, unless the specific means or methods of collection breach applicable international legal obligations. This aligns with the consistent state practice spanning over 70 years. Drafters of the manual have not hesitated to address some controversial issues. For instance, Rule 26 concerning self-defence in and from outer space recognises the right of anticipatory self-defence against any activity that constitutes an imminent armed attack. Therefore, it extends beyond Article 51 of the United Nations Charter, acknowledging substantial state practice supported by *opinio juris*, which demonstrates the existence of such a right under customary international law. The manual is expected to provide practical guidance for space law practitioners in government, academia, non-governmental organisations, the private sector, and other fields.[44] Only time will tell whether this manual and, for that

42 David Koplow, 'In the Woomera Manual, International Law Meets Military Space Activities', *Just Security*, 12 (2024). https://www.justsecurity.org/100043/woomera-manual-international-law-military-space/ Accessed 25 November 2025.

43 Ibid.

44 Koplow, 'In the Woomera Manual'.

matter, the MILAMOS, will succeed in reshaping state practice in the space domain in response to the increasing challenges posed by space weaponisation. It is worth noting that both initiatives have received praise from experts as outstanding efforts of vital importance that will support future legal developments in outer space, especially those of a military nature.[45]

Proposals made by experts

Given that the weaponisation of space is a significant challenge for space exploration, some experts have proposed solutions to address this complex issue. A brief review of some of these proposals is provided here.

Sergio Marchisio recognises that establishing legally binding norms to complement the current international legal framework and tackle the challenges of space weaponisation would be challenging and time-consuming in the present situation.[46] However, a non-legally binding instrument grounded in fundamental principles and voluntary TCBM can serve as a short-term solution and an essential means of building trust and confidence among space actors.[47] This could result in increased commitments to arms control in outer space.[48] Nivedita Raju also advocates a similar approach, highlighting the virtues of the EU Code of Conduct for Outer Space Activities.[49] The 'soft law' approach definitely has some merit. It may be recalled that, in the early days of space exploration, the adoption of the Outer Space Treaty in 1967 and other treaties thereafter was preceded by a United Nations General Assembly resolution on the Declaration of Legal Principles, adopted unanimously in 1963. The EU Code of Conduct did not receive wider support, not because of significant issues with its content, but mainly because of its exclusive development and the forum in which it was adopted.

Nina Tannenwald, after emphasising the importance of a legal regime for space militarisation, refers to the framework and outcome of the United Nations Convention on the Law of the Sea of 1982 (UNCLOS III) and draws parallels between this treaty and a future regime for outer space.[50] After

45 Loon, 'Codifying *Jus in Bello Spatialis*', 14.

46 Sergio Marchisio, 'The Final Frontier: Prospects for Arms Control in Outer Space', *Global Security Policy Brief, European Leadership Network*, (July 2019), 56. http://www.jstor.com/stable/resrep22117 Accessed 25 November 2025.

47 Ibid.

48 Ibid.

49 Nivedita Raju, 'A Proposal for a Ban on Destructive Anti-Satellite Testing: A Role for the European Union?', *Non-Proliferation and Disarmament Papers*, 74 (2021), 14. https://www.sipri.org/publications/2021/eu-non-proliferation-and-disarmament-papers/proposal-ban-destructive-anti-satellite-testing-role-european-union Accessed 25 November 2025.

50 Nina Tannenwald, 'Law Versus Power on the High Frontier: The Case for a Rule Based Regime for Outer Space', *Yale Journal of International Law*, 29 (2004), 363–422. https://openyls.law.yale.edu/handle/20.500.13051/6495 Accessed 25 November 2025.

considering various approaches for developing a new legal regime, she proposes adopting a framework convention to establish a structure for further cooperation among the parties through monitoring and implementation procedures, data exchange, and facilitation of scientific research, while protocols would provide greater specificity in addressing individual issues.[51] This presupposes agreement on broad principles to be followed step-by-step, along with protocols for specific issues, something that has been tried in the fields of environmental protection and the regulation of conventional weapons. She also suggests complementing this approach with an international civil society campaign, such as the Ottawa Process, which led to the adoption of the Treaty on Anti-Personnel Landmines in 1997.[52]

Brian Chow describes co-orbital ASAT satellites as 'space stalkers' or, technically, 'proximity operations', and advocates for banning satellites that come too close to another country's satellites beyond a certain threshold.[53] He recommends control measures to improve deterrence and defence against not only 'space stalkers' but also various traditional and emerging threats.[54] His suggestion is to establish a 'foundational' or 'core' treaty, to which additional control measures can be added. These include facilitating the monitoring of active debris removal and on-orbit servicing spacecraft, prohibiting simultaneous unmanned proximity operations tests, banning ground-launched ballistic-missile ASAT weapons tests, and mandating prelaunch inspections for all space launches.[55] Furthermore, he suggests addressing the other six types of space weapons: Space-based ASAT weapons with less than 10 km range; space-based defensive weapons with less than 10 km range; space-based ASAT weapons with 10 km or more range; space-based defensive weapons with 10 km or more range; ground-launched ASAT weapons; and space-based weapons aimed at terrestrial targets.[56] This should be achieved gradually. This method, like the one proposed by Tannenwald, is called a 'hybrid approach' by Chow. If successful, it would effectively address all issues related to space weaponisation and self-defence in outer space.

Given the deadlock in the Conference on Disarmament over PPWT and other proposals, Paul Meyer suggests adopting an Optional Protocol to the Outer Space Treaty to prevent an arms race in outer space.[57] He proposes that the negotiation process for an optional protocol could utilise existing UN

51 Ibid., 420.

52 Ibid., 421.

53 Brian G. Chow, 'Space Arms Control: A Hybrid Approach', *Strategic Studies Quarterly*, 12 (2018), 107–32. https://www.jstor.org/stable/26430818 Accessed 25 November 2025.

54 Ibid., 120.

55 Ibid., 120–6.

56 Ibid., 126.

57 Paul Meyer, 'Could an Optional Protocol Be the Way to Stop Weaponisation of Outer Space?', *International Journal*, 76 (2021), 336.

mechanisms, either through the Committee on the Peaceful Uses of Outer Space or, if consensus cannot be achieved in that body, via a UN General Assembly-mandated procedure, or even through an Ad Hoc diplomatic conference.[58] Meyer is optimistic that an optional protocol extending the Outer Space Treaty's ban on weapons of mass destruction to all types of weaponry should not be overly complicated to draft.[59] He has some suggestions for tackling complex issues, such as defining a 'space weapon' and verifying the proposed ban.[60]

Brian Britt has proposed three interim measures to address the challenges associated with space weaponisation, towards more comprehensive agreements in the future.[61] The first is an international moratorium on kinetic ASAT weapons tests that generate debris; the second involves transparency and confidence-building measures at a specific orbital altitude, in the absence of a comprehensive definition of space weapons; and the third highlights the need to identify abnormal behaviour, enabling warnings of and protection against space threats.[62] He acknowledges that these proposals are only temporary and partial, as a comprehensive agreement on space weaponisation is currently unfeasible due to significant disagreements among groups of states.[63]

Concluding remarks

As the United States and the Soviet Union intensified their research on new space-based weapons, the global community, alarmed by this development, began calling for legal measures to prevent the weaponisation of space. Many countries proposed measures within the United Nations to prevent the escalation of the arms race into outer space. Meanwhile, other nations joined the space community and also started developing technologies aimed at space weaponisation. Since the 1990s and 2000s, China and Russia have led the way in proposing specific measures, including the adoption of a binding treaty on space weaponisation. The Group of 21 countries supported this initiative.

The United States and other Western countries have numerous reservations about the 2014 draft treaty on PPWT by China and Russia. Their concerns mainly focus on defining space weapons, challenges in

58 Ibid.

59 Ibid.

60 Ibid., 337–8.

61 Brian Britt, 'The PPWT and Ongoing Challenges to Arms Control in Space', *Joint Force Quarterly*, 113 (2024), 83. https://digitalcommons.ndu.edu/joint-force-quarterly/vol113/iss1/13/ Accessed 25 November 2025.

62 Ibid., 83–4.

63 Ibid., 85.

verification and monitoring, exclusion of terrestrial space weapons from the treaty's scope, and the non-prohibition of possession, testing, production, and stockpiling of the weapons covered by the draft. They also raise concerns regarding the use of force in outer space in accordance with the United Nations Charter and other anomalies. Currently, a deadlock persists in the Conference on Disarmament, which has been discussing PAROS since 1982. The United Nations General Assembly has attempted to follow the recommendations of the Group of Governmental Experts, but without success. Some academic institutions and individual experts have also put forward various proposals. Nonetheless, the key question remains: Are there any prospects for tangible progress, grounded in the rule of law, to address the challenges posed by impending space weaponisation, or should we wait and see, perhaps until a misadventure causes catastrophic consequences? This question will be examined in the next and final chapter of this work.

References

Britt B., 'The PPWT and Ongoing Challenges to Arms Control in Space', *Joint Force Quarterly*, 113 (2024), 83. https://digitalcommons.ndu.edu/joint-force-quarterly/vol113/iss1/13/ Accessed 25 November 2025.

Centner C., 'One Small Step for Man, One Giant Problem for Mankind', *International and Comparative Law Review*, 32 (2022). https://international-and-comparative-law-review.law.miami.edu/one-small-step-for-man-one-giant-problem-for-mankind Accessed 25 November 2025.

Chow B. G., 'Space Arms Control: A Hybrid Approach', *Strategic Studies Quarterly*, 12 (2018), 107–32. https://www.jstor.org/stable/26430818 Accessed 25 November 2025.

European Union External Action, 'Diplomatic Service of the European Union'. https://www.eeas.europa.eu/sites/default/files/space_code_conduct_draft_vers_31-march-2014_en.pdf Accessed 25 November 2025.

Johnson C., 'Draft International Code of Conduct for Outer Space Activities: Fact Sheet', *Secure World Foundation*, (February 2014). https://swfound.org/media/166384/swf_draft_international_code_of_conduct_for_outer_space_activities_fact_sheet_february_2014.pdf Accessed 25 November 2025.

Koplow D., 'In the Woomera Manual, International Law Meets Military Space Activities', *Just Security*, 12 (2024). https://www.justsecurity.org/100043/woomera-manual-international-law-military-space/ Accessed 25 November 2025.

Loon F., 'Codifying *Jus in Bello Spatialis*: The Space Law of Tomorrow', *Strategic Studies Quarterly*, 15 (2021), 10–27.

Marchisio S., 'The Final Frontier: Prospects for Arms Control in Outer Space', *Global Security Policy Brief, European Leadership Network*, (July 2019), 53–64. http://www.jstor.com/stable/Resrep22117 Accessed 25 November 2025.

McGill Institute of Air and Space Law, https://www.mcgill.ca/iasl/projects/mcgill-manual Accessed 25 November 2025.

Meyer P., 'The CD and PAROS: A Short History', *CD Discussion Series*, UNIDIR, (April 2011).

Meyer P., 'Could an Optional Protocol Be the Way to Stop Weaponisation of Outer Space?', *International Journal*, 76 (2021), 332–9. https://journals.sagepub.com/doi/full/10.1177/00207020211020521 Accessed 25 November 2025.

Raju N., 'A Proposal for a Ban on Destructive Anti-Satellite Testing: A Role for the European Union?', *Non-Proliferation and Disarmament Papers*, 74 (2021), 1–16. https://www.sipri.org/publications/2021/eu-non-proliferation-and-disarmament-papers/proposal-ban-destructive-anti-satellite-testing-role-european-union Accessed 25 November 2025.

Stephens D. and Jarose J., *The Woomera Manual and Military Space Activities and Operations*. West Point: Lieber Institute, 2024. https://lieber.westpoint.edu/woomera-manual-military-space-activities-operations/ Accessed 25 November 2025.

Tannenwald N., 'Law Versus Power on the High Frontier: The Case for a Rule Based Regime for Outer Space', *Yale Journal of International Law*, 29 (2004), 363–422. https://openyls.law.yale.edu/handle/20.500.13051/6495 Accessed 25 November 2025.

The UN Chronicle, 10/11 (1984).

UN COPUOS, *Report of the Twenty-Seventh Session of the COPUOS*, Vienna, (12–21 June 1984).

UN Doc. A/AC.105/PV. 220.

UN Doc. A/Res/65/68.

UN Doc. A/Res/68/189.

UN Doc. A/Res/69/32.

UN Doc. A/Res/77/41.

UN Doc. A/Res/79/20.

UN Doc. CD/1606.

UN Doc. CD/1679.

UN Doc. CD/1839.

UN Doc. CD/1847.

UN Doc. CD/1985.

UN Doc. CD/1998.

UN Doc. CD/2078.

UN Doc. GE-PAROS/2024/CRP.4.

UN Docs. A/Res/36/97.

UN Docs. A/Res/36/99.

UN GA Res. A/79/512.

United Nations, 'For Second Time Since Late April Security Council Fails to Adopt First-Ever Resolution on Preventing Arms Race in Outer Space'. https://press.un.org/en/2024/sc15700.doc.htm Accessed 29 November 2025.

United Nations, 'Security Council Fails to Adopt First-Ever Resolution on Arms Race in Outer Space, Due to Negative Vote by Russian Federation'. https://press.un.org/en/2024/sc15678.doc.htm Accessed 29 November 2025.

United Nations Department for Disarmament Affairs, *The United Nations Disarmament Yearbook*, Volume 7. New York: United Nations, 1982.

United Nations Office for Disarmament Affairs, https://disarmament.unoda.org/topics/outerspace/paros-gge/#:~:text=In%20accordance%20with%20operative%20paragraph,ended%20intersessional%20informal%20consultative%20meeting%2C Accessed 25 November 2025.

United Nations Office for Disarmament Affairs, https://meetings.unoda.org/gge-paros/group-of-governmental-experts-on-further-practical-measuRes-for-the-prevention-of-an-arms-race-in-outer-space-2023 Accessed 25 November 2025.

6 Conclusions and recommendations

Early developments in space law relied on mutual understanding and a spirit of cooperation between the two superpowers of the time, despite their fierce rivalry for dominance in space. Both recognised the dangers of having weapons of mass destruction in outer space, always threatening them and their allies. As a result, they did not hesitate to prohibit the deployment of such weapons in outer space. After this, they also recognised the need for additional norms covering issues such as space accidents, liability for damage, identification of space objects, astronauts in distress, and resources of celestial bodies, among others. They agreed to develop new standards to address these concerns. However, since 1979, no major space treaty has been adopted. A common challenge in reaching an arms control agreement is due to a lack of political will and insufficient trust among states.[1] This pertains to the concern that a legally binding treaty on space weaponisation might disadvantage states that become parties and commit to the norms. Conversely, states that are not parties and do not conform to the norms might be able to act outside the treaty's scope without significant consequences.[2] For example, the United States has observed that although China and Russia have been making proposals at the Conference on Disarmament to initiate negotiations on a new treaty banning the deployment of weapons in outer space, both have been developing terrestrial ASAT weapons and conducting tests to that end.[3]

Regulating space weapons cannot be considered separately from terrestrial military preparedness. It is said that between 1957 and 1990, nearly 70 per cent of all satellites launched were utilised to support terrestrial military activities, particularly nuclear forces.[4] Today, it is difficult to determine how many satellites support terrestrial military activity, as most satellites serve

1 UNIDIR, Outer Space Security Conference Report, (2021), 15.
2 Ibid.
3 UN Doc. CD/2129, 2.
4 Kaitlyn Johnson, 'A Balance of Instability: Effects of a Direct-Ascent Anti-Satellite Weapons Ban on Nuclear Stability', *Occasional Paper*, Project on Nuclear Issues, Centre for Strategic and International Studies, (21 October 2020), 4. https://aerospace.csis.

DOI: 10.4324/9781003754428-7

both civilian and military purposes. During the Cold War period, both superpowers launched reconnaissance satellites into orbit to collect intelligence on each other's missile forces, including production sites, known launch locations, and missile defence systems.[5] They also used communications satellites to ensure nuclear command and control, enabling rapid, direct message transmission during a crisis.[6] These military uses of outer space have become acceptable to the majority of states through extensive state practice, leading to the formation of a customary law norm. Satellite reconnaissance indirectly contributes to maintaining international peace and security by assisting in verifying arms control agreements. Other military uses of outer space, such as military communication, can be justified by claiming that every state is entitled to use its technological capacity to enhance its preparedness for defence and security. However, the international community is deeply concerned about the potential expansion of an arms race into outer space. The plans of some nations to develop and deploy a variety of weapons in outer space are highly alarming.

Regarding direct-ascent kinetic ASAT weapons tests, two conclusions are inescapable. First, such tests produce significant space debris. Second, space debris presents a clear threat to satellites of all nations, both civilian and military. To protect the space environment and ensure that peaceful exploration of outer space continues unhindered, banning the testing, development, possession, and use of direct-ascent kinetic ASAT weapons is essential. The United States and its allies seem to support this not out of altruism, but because they have already developed, or can develop, non-kinetic ASAT weapons, such as directed energy weapons, to maintain strategic stability. Conversely, China and Russia – the two nations that threaten the United States' space assets – are not yet confident in non-kinetic ASAT capabilities.[7] As a result, they are developing direct-ascent kinetic ASAT weapons and therefore do not want to close that option off. Their proposals on PPWT explicitly exclude terrestrial ASAT weapons. They are both aware of how much the United States depends on space assets for various civilian and military space activities. To exploit this vulnerability and maintain strategic stability, neither wishes to relinquish its kinetic ASAT capabilities. It is also thought that China and Russia regard kinetic ASAT weapons as an equaliser, enabling them to compensate for a relative conventional disadvantage against the United States and its allies.[8] Both countries are also concerned about the United States' deployment of

org/a-balance-of-instability-effects-of-a-direct-ascent-anti-satellite-weapons-ban-on-nuclear-stability/ Accessed 25 November 2025.

5 Ibid.

6 Ibid., 4–5.

7 Ibid., 9.

8 Britt, 'The PPWT and Ongoing Challenges', 82.

anti-ballistic missile systems in outer space. Since the United States withdrew from the 1972 Anti-Ballistic Missile Treaty in 2002, there have been no legal restrictions on deploying such systems in space. Even the Outer Space Treaty does not prohibit this, as anti-ballistic missile weapons might not be classified as 'weapons of mass destruction' under Article IV of the Treaty.

One of the main conclusions of this work is that nuclear weapons that are not weapons of mass destruction can be placed in outer space, but not on celestial bodies. As noted earlier, some states are planning to develop nuclear-powered X-ray laser weapons that may be deployed in outer space. According to some commentators and states, nuclear-powered X-ray lasers cannot be placed in outer space in view of the treaty's prohibition on placing 'in orbit around the Earth any objects carrying nuclear weapons or any other kinds of weapons of mass destruction'.

One difficulty in regulating space weapons is reconciling them with the right of self-defence. Under existing international law, a state may use military force against its adversary's space assets in self-defence if the conditions for exercising this right are fulfilled. Is it possible to designate the entire outer space as a zone where no military force can be employed, even for self-defence? It appears unlikely that states will agree to such a comprehensive ban. They may agree to ban the stationing of weapons in outer space but retain the right to develop and deploy Earth-to-space weapons, claiming they are necessary for self-defence. Applying the logic of the International Court of Justice in the *Nuclear Weapons Advisory Opinion*, if use of nuclear weapons may be justified 'in an extreme circumstance of self-defence, in which the very survival of a State would be at stake', it is possible to justify the use of military force against a hostile satellite if the necessity of self-defence so demands.[9] As mentioned earlier, both the 2008 and 2014 China-Russia joint drafts of PPWT emphasise that the right to individual and collective self-defence, as outlined in Article 51 of the UN Charter, remains unaffected by the draft treaties.[10]

Regulation of space militarisation: The way forward

Today, the primary concern of the international community is how to address the dangers posed by non-mass-destruction weapons in outer space and to protect its space assets against attacks from terrestrial space weapons. The issue of regulating space weaponisation, including the development of terrestrial space weapons, has been on the international community's agenda for over 50 years. From time to time, various proposals have emerged in different forums. No proposal, however comprehensive, practical, or perfect, will be

9 *Legality of the Threat or Use of Nuclear Weapons Advisory Opinion*, 8 July 1996, ICJ Rep. 1996, para. 105.

10 Article V of the 2008 draft and Article IV of the 2014 draft.

helpful unless the leading space powers accept it. Currently, the international community's focus is on the 2014 PPWT proposal, jointly submitted by China and Russia. As mentioned earlier, the proposal is not acceptable to the United States for reasons previously discussed.[11] Under these circumstances, the following three scenarios can be considered:

1. The U.S. and its allies are persuaded to consider the current PPWT draft with certain modifications to make it acceptable to them and other space powers.
2. The status quo continues until a new draft treaty that is acceptable to most countries, including all the major space powers, is developed and thoroughly debated.
3. The deadlock remains unresolved. Meanwhile, some nations are progressing in both land-based and space-based ASAT and BMD technologies.

The second and third scenarios are less than ideal, particularly regarding safety and security in outer space. Military space powers' primary concern is that their satellites, used for command, control, communication, and intelligence gathering for nuclear or other military operations, are highly vulnerable to hostile interference, ranging from jamming to physical destruction. Regulating military activities in outer space is a complex task. It is almost impossible to persuade leading space powers to agree on a comprehensive and legally binding instrument that addresses all issues related to the militarisation of outer space. Therefore, the author suggests a step-by-step approach that could involve a combination of unilateral commitments, 'soft-law' measures such as non-binding resolutions or declarations by key United Nations bodies, and binding treaties when consensus among leading space powers can be reached.

There are some subtle signs of possible positive developments. A study commissioned by the Secure World Foundation concluded in October 2023 that a consensus is forming against destructive ASAT missile tests.[12] Furthermore, there appears to be a diminishing contrast between the two approaches of norms and legally binding instruments in addressing space security.[13]

The initial step in this process was taken in 1967 by prohibiting the placement of weapons of mass destruction in outer space and on celestial bodies. Nearly 60 years have elapsed since then, during which there have been unprecedented advances in the field of space militarisation. The international

11 *Supra*, Chapter 5, at 95–6.

12 Chiang Wei Sooi, 'Direct-Ascent Anti-Satellite Tests: State Positions on the Moratorium, UNGA Resolution, and Lessons for the Future', *Report of the Secure World Foundation*, (October 2023), V. https://swfound.org/media/207711/direct-ascent-antisatellite-missile-tests_state-positions-on-the-moratorium-unga-resolution-and-lessons-for-the-future.pdf Accessed 25 November 2025.

13 Ibid.

community agrees that the arms race should not extend into outer space. However, the main issue is how to accomplish this. After reviewing technological advances, current proposals, and the stances of different groups of states, the following course of action might be helpful.

(a) The United States is planning to develop BMD weapons for deployment in outer space. However, it is quite likely that any attempt to deploy such systems in outer space may not be attractive diplomatically or strategically. Politically, because it would initiate the weaponisation of space – an action regarded as harmful by the international community; strategically, because it would prompt the United States' adversaries, primarily China and Russia, to develop and deploy similar systems in space. This would undoubtedly undermine strategic stability.[14] They may also respond by developing new and additional types of long-range ballistic missiles, as well as rockets that follow non-ballistic trajectories.[15] Nonetheless, President Trump remains committed to advancing his 'Golden Dome' project.[16] This is the main reason the United States vetoed a Security Council resolution in May 2024 that would have banned the stationing of all types of weapons in outer space. Nevertheless, strategists have repeatedly advocated that the United States should take a proactive role in developing legal standards for regulating space weaponisation.[17] One of the main concerns of China and Russia is that BMD weapons can be easily adapted for ASAT applications.

(b) As previously mentioned, there have been several significant developments concerning a unilateral moratorium on ASAT weapons tests so far.[18] In this context, one possible measure is for the General Assembly to adopt a resolution to recommend a moratorium on both space-based and terrestrial ASAT weapons tests. As noted earlier, Brian Britt has suggested a moratorium on ASAT weapons tests that generate space debris as an interim measure.[19] Nevertheless, such a moratorium should encompass all ASAT weapons tests, not only those that produce space debris. This would go well beyond the UN General Assembly resolution calling for a moratorium solely on direct-ascent ASAT weapons tests.[20]

(c) The UN General Assembly could take the initiative to develop some 'soft law' norms to address space militarisation. It could adopt a 'Declaration

14 John Harper, 'Would Space Based Interceptors Spark a New Arms Race?', *National Defence*, 103 (2019), 26. https://www.jstor.org/stable/10.2307/27022548 Accessed 25 November 2025.

15 Ibid.

16 *Supra*, Chapter 3, at 48–9.

17 Kenneth S. Blazejewski, 'Space Weaponization and US-China Relations', *Strategic Studies Quarterly*, 2 (2008), 34.

18 *Supra*, Chapter 5, at 97–8.

19 Britt, 'The PPWT and Ongoing Challenges', 83.

20 UN Doc. A/RES/77/41.

of Principles of International Law for Safety and Security in Outer Space and on Celestial Bodies'. Such a declaration might recognise existing legal norms and explicitly legitimise the use of outer space for specific military activities that have gained widespread acceptance through extensive state practice, such as the use of military satellites for communication, reconnaissance, and military meteorology. It could acknowledge that placing any weapons – both weapons of mass destruction and non-mass destruction – in outer space would constitute a threat to international peace and security within the meaning of Article 2(4) of the United Nations Charter. It might recommend a moratorium on deploying such weapons in outer space and reaffirm the moratorium on space-based as well as terrestrial ASAT weapons tests, as suggested in paragraph (a) above, until a comprehensive treaty addressing space weaponisation is adopted. Such a declaration will undoubtedly lay the groundwork for a future comprehensive treaty.

(d) The Conference on Disarmament may be urged to adopt a recommendatory resolution on 'Transparency and Confidence-Building Measures' (TCBM). As noted earlier, in July 2013, the United Nations General Assembly urged members to implement the TCBM recommended by the Group of Governmental Experts established to identify them.[21] That process may be revitalised and resumed at the Conference on Disarmament. As it stands, the Group of Governmental Experts' achievements were a rare success. Many states are in favour of implementing TCBM. The proposed China-Russia joint PPWT of 2014 also encourages States Parties to implement TCBM voluntarily.[22] The United States strongly advocates for TCBM. A strong recommendation from the Conference on Disarmament would be a positive step towards regulating military activities in outer space. Admittedly, the acceptance and implementation of TCBM are complex and contentious issues, heavily influenced by national security interests competing with safety concerns in outer space. The TCBM process is a component of the broader idea of responsible behaviour in outer space. It is believed that, despite years of deadlock over a legally binding multilateral treaty on space weaponisation and non-binding international instruments aimed at fostering norms of responsible behaviour, there have been some promising efforts in recent decades.[23] With increased diplomatic efforts, though challenging, it is possible to persuade major space powers to reach a consensus on the content and implementation of TCBM.

21 *Supra*, Chapter 5, at 96.

22 Article V of the draft treaty.

23 See generally, Bruce McClintock, Katie Feistel, Douglas C. Ligor, and Kathryn O'Conner, *Responsible Space Behaviour for New Space Era: A Report* (Santa Monica: RAND Corporation, 2021). https://www.jstor.org/stable/resrep30909.3 Accessed 25 November 2025.

(e) One particular TCBM that could be considered in this context is the adoption of a resolution by the UN General Assembly on the declaration of 'Exclusive Space Security Zones'. All major space powers operate high-altitude military satellites that are essential for their national security, including nuclear deterrence. If a hostile state manoeuvres its satellite near such critical satellites, it might be seen as a sign of preparation for an attack. Such a misunderstanding could cause increased tension and the potential use of force against the hostile satellite, possibly sparking a wider conflict. To prevent any risk of attack on critical satellites, it has been suggested that space powers might be persuaded to declare 'keep out zones' around these satellites.[24] Military exclusion zones are recognised by laws governing land, naval, and aerial warfare.[25] Admittedly, there are some challenges in reaching a consensus on 'Exclusive Space Security Zones', particularly regarding their reconciliation with the space law principle of non-appropriation, their duration, and geographic scope, among other issues. However, given the changed realities of the modern space age, such obstacles are not insurmountable if most space powers recognise their importance for space security and their national interests. Some discussion is already underway on this concept.[26] The concept should be refined in consultation with all space powers, preferably under the auspices of the Conference on Disarmament.

(f) Considering the disagreement among states regarding the deployment of nuclear-powered X-ray laser weapons in outer space, it is advisable that the General Assembly or the Conference on Disarmament adopt a resolution imposing a moratorium on the stationing of any nuclear weapons in outer space, whether they are weapons of mass destruction or not. This will help resolve the ambiguity surrounding the deployment of non-mass-destruction weapons in outer space. If such a resolution gains broader support, especially from the key space powers, it can eventually be transformed into a binding protocol to the Outer Space Treaty. Although Russia and China are

24 George Perkovich, 'Engaging China on Strategic Stability and Mutual Vulnerability', *Carnegire Endowment for International Peace: A Working Paper*, (October 2022), 17. https://carnegie-production-assets.s3.amazonaws.com/static/files/Perkovich-Engaging_China.pdf Accessed 25 November 2025.

25 See generally, Cole M. Mooty, Robert A. Bettinger, and Mark G. Reith, 'Domain Restriction Zones: An Evolution of Military Exclusion Zones', *Air and Space Operations Review*, 2 (2023), 20–36.

26 For example, see Lucas Mallowan, Lucien Rapp, and Maria Topka, 'Reinventing Treaty Compliant "Safety Zones" in the Context of Space Sustainability', *Journal of Space Safety Engineering*, 8 (2021), 155–66. https://www.sciencedirect.com/science/article/abs/pii/S2468896721000379 and Jessy Kate Schingler, 'Imagining Safety Zones: Implications and Open Questions', *The Space Review*, (8 June 2020). https://www.thespacereview.com/article/3962/1 Accessed 25 November 2025.

currently opposed to such a resolution, it could be seen as a step toward banning all kinds of weapons in outer space, as these two space powers have insisted.

(g) The lack of a clear boundary between airspace and outer space poses significant challenges for military operations. States involved in various types of military activities in outer space should respect other states' airspace sovereignty. Otherwise, confrontation and conflict in outer space and elsewhere are likely to arise. Therefore, states must endeavour to establish an acceptable legal definition of outer space.

(h) Negotiating a binding treaty on 'Space Weapons' – both space-based and terrestrial – would be the ideal yet most challenging step. This can be pursued once the earlier steps are completed and approximately 5 to 10 years have elapsed. It is anticipated that these steps would lead to a legally binding instrument. Extensive debate and discussion have occurred regarding the PPWT draft submitted jointly by China and Russia in 2014 under the auspices of the Conference on Disarmament. As noted earlier, there are significant differences of opinion among groups of states regarding the draft treaty. It is expected that the steps outlined previously will encourage states to soften their hard-line positions, resolve their differences, and reach a consensus. However, in the present context, this appears improbable. Major space powers have significant concerns regarding the safety and security of their critical space assets. Unless these concerns are satisfactorily addressed, genuine progress is unlikely.

(i) The civil society campaigns launched by some non-governmental organisations must be strengthened and supported widely.[27] Such initiatives have demonstrated their effectiveness in persuading the international community to adopt treaties such as the Ottawa Anti-personnel Landmines Treaty, the Rome Statute on the International Criminal Court, and the Arms Trade Treaty.

All things considered, regulating military activities in outer space faces numerous formidable challenges. Realistically, only gradual progress can be made in the coming decades unless states are prepared to move away from their rigid positions. This will only occur if their national security concerns are addressed. Until then, the current deadlock will persist. However, the duration of this remains uncertain, despite the rapid pace at which space weaponisation is likely to accelerate in the coming years.

27 See generally, the work of agencies such as the Global Network Against Weapons and Nuclear Power in Space, Women's International League for Peace and Freedom, Secure World Foundation, and Project Ploughshares.

References

Blazejewski K. S., 'Space Weaponization and US-China Relations', *Strategic Studies Quarterly*, 2 (2008), 33–55.

Britt B., 'The PPWT and Ongoing Challenges to Arms Control in Space', *Joint Force Quarterly*, 113 (2024), 80–5. https://digitalcommons.ndu.edu/joint-force-quarterly/vol113/iss1/13/ Accessed 25 November 2025.

Harper J., 'Would Space Based Interceptors Spark a New Arms Race?', *National Defence*, 103 (2019), 26–7. https://www.jstor.org/stable/10.2307/27022548 Accessed 25 November 2025.

Johnson K., 'A Balance of Instability: Effects of a Direct-Ascent Anti-Satellite Weapons Ban on Nuclear Stability', *Occasional Paper*, Project on Nuclear Issues, Centre for Strategic and International Studies, (21 October 2020), 1–12. https://aerospace.csis.org/a-balance-of-instability-effects-of-a-direct-ascent-anti-satellite-weapons-ban-on-nuclear-stability/ Accessed 25 November 2025.

Legality of the Threat or Use of Nuclear Weapons, Advisory Opinion, 8 July 1996, ICJ Rep. 1996.

Mallowan L., Rapp L. and Topka M., 'Reinventing Treaty Compliant "Safety Zones" in the Context of Space Sustainability', *Journal of Space Safety Engineering*, 8 (2021), 155–66. https://www.sciencedirect.com/science/article/abs/pii/S2468896721000379

McClintock B., Feistel K., Ligor D. C. et al., *Responsible Space Behaviour for New Space Era: A Report*. Santa Monica: RAND Corporation, 2021. https://www.jstor.org/stable/resrep30909.3 Accessed 25 November 2025.

Mooty C. M., Bettinger R. A. and Reith M. G., 'Domain Restriction Zones: An Evolution of Military Exclusion Zones', *Air and Space Operations Review*, 2 (2023), 20–36.

Perkovich G., 'Engaging China on Strategic Stability and Mutual Vulnerability', *Carnegie Endowment for International Peace: A Working Paper*, (October 2022), 17. https://carnegie-production-assets.s3.amazonaws.com/static/files/Perkovich-Engaging_China.pdf Accessed 25 November 2025.

Schingler J. K., 'Imagining Safety Zones: Implications and Open Questions', *The Space Review*, (8 June 2020). https://www.thespacereview.com/article/3962/1 Accessed 25 November 2025.

Sooi C. W., 'Direct-Ascent Anti-Satellite Tests: State Positions on the moratorium, UNGA Resolution, and Lessons for the Future', *Report of the Secure World Foundation*, (October 2023), V. https://swfound.org/media/207711/direct-ascent-antisatellite-missile-tests_state-positions-on-the-moratorium-unga-resolution-and-lessons-for-the-future.pdf Accessed 25 November 2025.

UN Doc. A/Res/77/41.

UN Doc. CD/2129.

UNIDIR, Outer Space Security Conference Report, (2021), 15.

Index

Note: Page numbers followed by n indicate notes.

For Product Safety Concerns and Information please contact our EU representative GPSR@taylorandfrancis.com Taylor & Francis Verlag GmbH, Kaufingerstraße 24, 80331 München, Germany